It's a State of Mind presents

Remember The Mission
Learn – Grow – Repeat

James Boardman

FUZZY
FLAMINGO

First published in 2021 by Fuzzy Flamingo

ISBN: 978-1-7399631-8-7

Editing and design by Fuzzy Flamingo
www.fuzzyflamingo.co.uk

A catalogue for this book is available from the British Library.

Disclaimer

This book is designed to provide helpful information on the subjects discussed. It is general reference information which should not be used to diagnose any medical problem and is not intended as a substitute for consulting with a medical or professional practitioner. Some names and identifying details have been changed to protect the privacy of individuals.

I'd like to dedicate this book to all those men and women who have fallen serving our country, and their families left behind. The ultimate sacrifice.

Contents

1

The Untold Truth

Heard it all before

Another self-help book, another attempt to try and find an answer to helping you change. Why are you here? What needs to change? And why do you need it?

I've been where you are right now – a lost soul, a lost identity, confused about what's next in life. The world can often seem overwhelming and cruel as you pursue happiness and fulfilment.

In writing this book, I have attempted to be as straight to the point as possible, based on my own personal experiences but also from my work with thousands of other men.

But I think it's only right to point out from the off that if you find it difficult to face the truth, not only is this book not for you, but you'll *never* be ready to change.

When are you going to stop fucking around, mate? When are you going to realise that your life matters and means something, that *you* mean something? When are you going to realise that you can't keep making the same BS excuses to justify the lack of action going on in your life?

You deserve better! Yes, *you* deserve better! And if you want something to change, then you'll need to hear this, because I'm not going to give you a lot of fluffy crap and tell you you're doing okay. I'm going to tell you straight what you're doing wrong – and, more importantly, what to do about it!

> January 1st – the beginning of a new year – is a classic example of when I hear most of the BS about changing.

'New year, new me.' 'This is the first day of my new life.' 'I'm desperate to change.' But however much you say you want to change yourself, I know it's a load of shit! Remember, I'm not trying to be the negative guy here, and I love the optimism and the fire, but I've seen and heard all of these comments and sentiments before. Sadly, though, it ends up being constant chatter about change… and nothing to show for it.

Think

Think about every time that you've said you are going to change. It's usually a Monday, as it's the start of the week; or the start of the month; or when you've had a health scare; or been on the piss all weekend and you're feeling rough; or maybe something has triggered an emotional response in you, such as a death in the family, which has made you realise that health is important; or you were maybe inspired by someone else's story. Who knows what's triggered the impulsive response to say you'll change, but you and I both know it's all been said before.

Think about how many times you've been to the gym since you took out the membership.

Think about how many times you left work on time and promised to be home for the family dinner, but never made it.

Think about how many times you press snooze on your alarm, or said you wouldn't have a drink, but slipped back into the habit of doing so.

Think about how many times you said you'd pay more attention to the kids or your wife, or both.

Think how many times you've said you're not eating crap any more.

As I'm guessing you can probably relate to quite a few of these statements, you should now be able to picture in your mind the things that aren't happening in your life, and the excuses we all make when we say we are going to do something yet nothing actually happens. How do the consequences of your lack of action make you feel, mate?

If I had a pound for every time I have heard a man say to me, *'I need to change my ways'* or *'things have to change'*, or *'I can't keep going on like this'*, I would literally be a millionaire.

So, when I get emails and messages from my clients – and even friends – about what they are going to do, I usually respond quite simply by saying, *'Show me, don't tell me!'*

Not backing yourself

It's as if you're making these statements out of habit, in response to recognising that you aren't where you want to be in life. But that's just an emotional response, like when you are hungry. You feel your tummy rumbling and the automatic response is, *'My God, I'm starving, I've got to eat.'* You look in the mirror and are unhappy with the way that you look, so the automatic response is to say, *'I hate my body, I'm going to the gym'* or *'I'm going for a run.'*

You might actually go for a run or a gym session, and you may ease the guilt for the day and feel like this is the change you desperately need... but how long does that last? I think you know in your own heart – not very long.

What's most eye-opening about this all, though, is the number of men who throw these statements around automatically or just out of habit, but don't back them up with actual action! And I have witnessed this myself through running my 5-day Fire It Up Challenge, which is a FREE 5-day course that I host to help men recognise where they are in their lives. It's hard to believe, but only 10-15% of the men who have registered actually show up to that FREE course. And that shocking statistic has been consistent over the last three years, since I wrote my first book, *It's a State of Mind*.

What makes matters worse is that there have been so many benefits for the thousands of men who did show up over those three years. Many have:

- regained control of their life
- saved their marriage or relationship
- seen a reduction in drinking alcohol
- prevented suicidal thoughts and actions, and
- formed stronger bonds with their children, partners, family, and friends

And by focusing attention on their habits, routines, and structure in the areas of life that matter, the course has helped many men to reduce their levels of anxiety and depression, and increase their understanding of these conditions.

Here's an example. On a course which consists of around 1000 men, roughly only 100-150 will show up. That's a staggering statistic when you look at what is being achieved by the ones who do show up, and the changes and breakthroughs being made. However, when I present this statistic in public forums or emails, it triggers negative emotions in some men. Quite often, a small percentage of them will lash out.

It can be hard to face the facts

It's a common response when you recognise yourself as one of those that don't show up, and you realise that you're full of shit. When the truth is being presented to them on a plate, some men just don't know how to respond. Being called out can be upsetting when you realise it's you that's being called out. It highlights the fact you've been neglecting yourself, and it can sting. But that truth can be used in two ways: many will use it as fire, to prompt them to take action; others will just see it as fuel to blame someone else. In fact, I'm willing to bet that some people will stop reading at this point and review this book as being negative. How can I be so sure? Because that's what happened with my first book.

The problem is that when the truth and the facts are presented, so many men just don't want to face up to them; in truth, nobody does. And I get that. After all, no one wants to accept that they aren't showing up and that they need to sort their shit out. So, I become the punchbag because I'm the one delivering the message. It's fine, though, because at least it means I've raised their awareness of the situation.

The question for them then becomes how they move forwards from having to face the hard truths. Their ego is going potty, so now what are they going to do?

The barriers to change

There seems to be a cycle, a pattern of habit-forming here. Most men want to change for the better and know they need to get out of the rut or hole they find themselves in. Some won't actually need to change too much, but just have to tweak some areas of their lives. Others will need to modify plenty, but won't or can't change for one reason or another. Those reasons will vary for each man and the way he sees the world, based on his own principles and values at that point in his life.

You might feel as if there's something missing in you, a huge hole somewhere. It's like you're missing a few jigsaw pieces from a puzzle, and you don't feel or can't be complete without all of the pieces coming together.

When the truth is black and white and not fluffed up, it tends to hurt when it's thrown in your face. So, how do you react? Some men like being told the situation as it is; some aren't used to it so aren't sure how to react; and some just don't understand it.

Let's be honest, there isn't enough straight talking out there. Too many have adopted a snowflake mentality these days, and when a man feels challenged, his chimp and ego feels the need to bite back. But straight talking doesn't mean being a dick; it just means you need to hear from someone else the things that you already say to yourself.

First, you need to stop being so easily offended. These 'home truths' need to be voiced to get you straight, and to stop you actually believing your own lies and BS. No one else is going to snap you out of that fairy-tale life you're living in, where you keep deluding yourself that '*everything is okay*'.

All that has done is to lull you into a false sense of security when, really, everything is NOT okay!

To be fair, that reality is hard for anyone to accept – even me! It was punishing on my ego and how I thought I was performing in life. I didn't realise I was at the bottom of the trenches, as that would make me vulnerable and weak. I was a Royal Marine Commando; surely we don't malfunction? Ego.

You have to want it

For the 85-90% of you that are making up excuses, not showing up, or complaining constantly about your life and telling yourself everything will eventually work out, I'm afraid I have some more bad news. No it won't, dude! There is no knight in shining armour, no magic wand, no cavalry coming to save you or do the work for you. To really want to change – well, that's down to you. In the three years that have passed since publishing my first book, I've come to learn that I can't help men who don't want to be helped or who aren't prepared to help themselves.

In fact, my two rules for working with me and to guarantee you'll make changes are:

1) To show the fuck up, 1% a day
2) To meet me halfway every day

There has to be a commitment from you to want to change. You have to get yourself out of bed, you have to put your own trainers on, you have to write your own plans, you have to show up to your relationship, and so on.

I know what you are thinking: *Where on earth do I start? I feel overwhelmed. I'm too far gone.*

Stop stressing! That is what this book is for – to help you.

Where are those guys?

You might wonder where exactly are those 85-90% of men who sign up but don't show up. They are busy, consumed, distracted, firefighting the days, weeks, and months – even years – that go by. They are being consumed by a mentality that blinds them to what's happening around them, burying their heads in the sand and ignoring the problem. Maybe some have accepted there is no way to change, no way out. I use the phrase 'they', but should I really be saying *you*?

How much longer will *you* hide behind the pain and suffering you go through internally and externally, as the reality of your truth stares at you so harrowingly in the mirror? You hear that little voice in the back of your mind that tells you it's going to be okay, you'll change soon, you'll get around to it. But will you really? How many tomorrows do you have left? And in the meantime, you passively continue to struggle, and those around you brace themselves for the ripple effects of your suffering as you fail to control your emotions.

Hot air

It's easy to get pumped up about life, right? To talk a good game, plan what you are going to do, how you are going to implement it all? It only takes a moment of motivation or to act on impulse after listening to a podcast, or watching a video, or seeing someone else do it.

In your mind, talking about what you want to do eases the guilt of the situation you are in. You might be feeling helpless, but convincing yourself through talk eases that guilt for a short period at least... until you don't actually follow up and produce the goods – again.

'Let's do this.'
'I'm going to gain more control of my life and plan out my day and week.'
'I'm going to get up at 5am and run five miles.'
'I'm not going to work at home tonight. I'm going to be present with the family.'

These are just some examples of what I see in the comments after a Rise To Thrive Show – the early morning show I run on Mondays, Wednesdays, and Fridays at 05.30 on The Man Coach Facebook page.

There's certainly lots of optimism, I'll give you that. I often see impulse comments like the above, amongst hundreds of other promises these guys make to themselves.

But what happens when the hype has died down and the motivation has disappeared?

What happens when it comes to implementing your plan and taking action?

What happened to all of that positive chat you made?

Why can't you do it, or maintain it?

Like many people, I'm sure you have started with good intentions, but how long do you actually last? A few days or weeks? Maybe even a month? But why don't you maintain that change consistently? Why is it not becoming an automatic and integrated part of your lifestyle to be able to show up with a minimum level of action that you know will benefit your main asset – you?

Building fundamentals

I want to share a story I heard when I was a kid, which I've never forgotten.

There were these two men: let's call them Mr Patient and Mr Impatient. Both were going to build their own house.

Mr Impatient was bragging about how he was going to build his house quickly. He was full of optimism and good intention.

Mr Patient didn't pay any attention to what was going on. He didn't feel the need to brag about what he was going to do, but just quietly went about his business of building the house, and doing what he said he was going to do.

Mr Impatient went straight into the project, all guns blazing, desperate to get his house up first. He wanted that instant gratification; he wanted instant results. And after one week, Mr Impatient had finished his house. It was tall, and everyone admired it.

Three weeks later, Mr Patient finished his house. It was equally as stunning, and he too was proud of what he had achieved.

A week later, there was a huge storm; the winds were

high and the rain poured in. Due to the high winds and storm conditions, Mr Impatient's house was seriously damaged, leaving it uninhabitable, and meaning that all of his early work had been for nothing.

So, why did Mr Impatient's house fall down? In the process of wanting to build the house as quickly as he could, he had taken shortcuts. He had failed to build his foundations strong enough to support the huge house he wanted.

Impatience leads to weak foundations

His desire for quick results and instant gratification meant he cut corners, which left his building vulnerable when the storm came. He missed key components in building his project, and that affected his structure.

Without the right foundations, his house was unable to stand upright when it faced adversity, external influences, and hardship. He had rushed the process, trying to do too much too soon, and as a result it all came crashing down on him.

Mr Patient, on the other hand, had taken his time to dig down before building up. He built up his foundations, which allowed him to construct a solid house that would withstand any storm over a long period of time. He had the long-term vision in mind when building his house, and knew that a quick fix approach would affect the stability of the building and the project.

Quick fix vs long-term solution

The moral of the story here reflects the pattern of so many men when it comes to change and self-development.

Mr Impatient rushed the process, based on his emotional state. Impulsive as ever, ego-driven, he wanted to change quickly. In the same way, most men are looking for the quick fixes in life, because they want to get out of their current situation as quickly as possible. And that's a natural reaction when you find yourself in a place you don't like. You automatically think: *How do I get out of this? And how quickly can I do it?*

I want to lose this belly 'quickly'; I want my business to grow 'quickly'; I want to improve my time management 'quickly'. Everything is about 'quick' these days, and often reflects people's expectations of where they should be and the timeframe in which they should achieve it.

Unfortunately, the vital foundations are overlooked and sacrificed for that instant gratification. Not many people are waking up and thinking where they could be and what they could achieve in one year, or three or five years. Instead, they wake up and want to achieve changes overnight, setting unrealistic expectations of themselves – and that is the first mistake to making change.

This doesn't benefit your long-term plan. Quick fixes only last a short amount of time before the realities of life pull you down, like a storm tearing down a house with weak foundations. And that's when you discover that those quick fixes just aren't strong enough to keep your house

– or you – up. They provide no foundations for you to remain in the game, so you stop trying to change for the better, and allow life to consume you once again.

As a result, the process collapses, as does all of the chat, desire, and want to change; the dreams and aspirations simply fade away. It becomes too hard to continue, so you go back to what you know best – firefighting the days, and running on your hamster wheel of doom. As a result, you're left feeling frustrated, low on confidence, and wondering if there is anything that will ever work to get you in the right place.

Building the foundations

Foundations are principles and values that you must learn, practise, and embrace, if you are going to build reliable, strong foundations for yourself. Think about when you learn to drive. At the very start of the process, you have no idea of what you are doing, but following the foundations helps build the process.

Mirror, signal, manoeuvre; looking in your mirrors every 15 seconds; driving within the speed limit; learning what the road signs mean.

After a period of time, these factors become second nature to you, and driving becomes a way of life. And I'll bet that when you get behind the wheel now, you don't even think about any of it. You instinctively know what to do, and follow a set of basic rules that keep you and others safe. (Of course, not everyone has great foundations when they drive, but you get my point!)

Now imagine if you tried to learn to drive by yourself, to rush the process, not hiring an instructor but maybe just following a YouTube video, or watching a friend. Do you think you'd have passed your test? Would you be likely to understand the foundations without guidance? I doubt it!

And self-development is exactly the same. It follows that same process of learn, grow, and repeat. Change isn't a light switch that, when flicked, works instantly. You need patience to build your foundations, to learn to take little steps, to chalk up small wins that eventually lead to you living a happier, more fulfilling life without even thinking about it… rather like getting behind the wheel of the car.

It's a journey of never-ending learning, and conditioning of the mind and emotions. And in this book I want to help you make sense of that journey, to help you go from being the procrastinator, to the action taker, to the Elite Operator. I want you to be battle-ready so that you are clear on your mission ahead, and can build on your foundations to construct the life you want.

Creating a mission for yourself and building foundations, principles, values, and character to achieve that mission, are what will help you change your thinking during this process. When it comes to you and your development, and the battle between quick fix and long-term happiness, remembering your mission – your North Star – is what will always emotionally bring you back to your path.

So, no more rushing the process; no more quick fixes; no more looking for the fastest change. It will now be a journey of just remembering the mission and working every day, forever, to achieve it.

2

Who the Fuck Am I to Tell You?

The black hole

If I were reading this book and not in an ideal place myself, I'd be thinking, *Who the fuck is this guy to tell me?* And that would be fair enough! It's all well and good preaching the gospel of what is and what isn't working, but you might well be wondering who I am to tell *you* what to do.

Some of you will know my story, but I've never truly laid it bare before. I realise, though, that if I want you to be vulnerable with me, then I have to be vulnerable with you. Many people see me as JB, the confident owner of multiple successful businesses, but believe me when I say it hasn't always been this way...

It was around 2.30am, sometime in November 2012, and it was pitch black outside. The room was extremely bright, as I didn't have a lampshade over the bulb. Sitting in my shorts, topless, I was uncontrollably stuck in a black hole of despair. And, boy, was I sinking fast. I didn't recognise who I was any more. There was this dark emotion; a storm of overthinking, creating extreme anxiety, which crippled my previously highly confident self.

I couldn't see any way out of this state of mind. There were a few positive aspects in my life, but I just couldn't manage to acknowledge or recognise them. At the same time, I had been managing really well to hide what was going on from the rest of the world.

What sat in front of me then was a bottle of whisky and numerous pills, which I hoped would just end the misery for good.

I had always said I could never take my own life, and that I would never try… Yet here I was, alone in that room, hoping this would do the trick.

When I think back to that time, I can't help but feel ashamed that I nearly went through with it. I know I shouldn't feel those emotions, but I do. That's just the reality of this situation.

Let me take you back a little to explain how I got to that life-changing evening for me – the journey over the years that built me up, then the changes to my life, and the reason I came crashing down.

I think it's important to understand the history to make sense of the present. But recapturing these years has been a tough write for me, and has brought back a flood of emotions that I haven't felt in years.

The start of my journey

In order to fully understand how I ended up getting to that point in my life where things were so bad that I felt I had to kill myself, I need to explain the journey I had been on for almost ten years. By understanding the shift in my state of mind, you will be able to see how I fell into that state.

In 2003, I arrived at Lympstone train station, where all potential Royal Marine Commandos begin, and I was led to the Foundation Block by a drill sergeant who scared the shit out of me. The Foundation Block was this huge complex where you lived for the first two weeks of Royal Marine Training, and if you've ever watched the movie *Full Metal Jacket,* it's just like their barracks. There's a huge room with 70 beds, sinks to scrub your kit, basic showers and toilets… and that's about it.

On the way from the station to the Foundation Block, I remember seeing these two strapping blokes with their green lids on – the coveted green beret, the trophy we all sought to wear as a Royal Marine Commando. They looked as hard as nails, rock solid, the kind of guys you wouldn't fuck with. And I've never forgotten them.

They created the vision of what I wanted to become, and I believe I was meant to see them on that first day while I was feeling really vulnerable and unsure that I was making the right decision to join the military. They gave me a picture of what I wanted to become, and it reassured me that I was taking the first step on the right path.

As time went on, whenever things got hard in training,

whenever I doubted myself, whenever I wanted to go home to the comfort of that shit, going-nowhere life I'd had before, I would think about those blokes, what my mission was, and imagine myself walking around in my green beret.

Every time it got tough, I thought of those lads – they were my emotional connection to what I was doing. The alternative was to go back to being manager of a top fast-food restaurant. No thanks; I had literally walked away from that chapter. I needed something so much more out of life, and had given up so much to be here, so I was determined that there would be no quitting.

Drifting

I joined the Royal Marines because I wanted to change my life, and I needed a challenge. Until that first day of training, I had been drifting, wanting the world but expecting everything to just come to me.

I wanted to achieve something huge, but I felt like a spare part until the moment I joined the military. I had nothing to show for my life, no real outcomes or achievements, and nothing to look forward to. So I decided to join the best military force in the world to see if I had what it took to get me through.

In preparation for starting training, I had spent seven months getting myself fit and ready. I was dedicated, committed, focused, and hungry, and more than ready to leave my life as I knew it. That included leaving behind my girlfriend (who went on to become my wife and mother to my oldest two children) and my friends, to step into the unknown.

Driven and passionate about my desire to change, I was totally focused and had just one outcome in mind – to become a Royal Marine Commando.

Why the military?

One of the major factors that convinced me to apply for the Royal Marines was watching one particular film. *Black Hawk Down* was a great movie, and I remember watching it at the cinema.

Just before the film started, there was a recruitment advert shown for the Royal Marines, and featured a young recruit running across open ground with his kit, then getting stuck inside a tunnel filled with water. It showed his resilience as he fought his way out, and was sent on his way.

The next scene showed the same guy on a boat, camouflaged up and with his green beret on, looking like an Elite Operator. In the space of that 120 seconds, I had just found what I needed in my life – a challenge, a change of environment, a need to be part of something!

And the movie itself only confirmed to me where my future was heading. I sat enthralled as I watched a group of men come together, bond, enjoy camaraderie, and get through a series of life-threatening struggles. And I wanted that! I'd never had that before, and I wanted to feel that bond with other blokes. I wanted to be part of something bigger than just my everyday life.

I wasn't even put off by the scenes of soldiers dying, or being shot at. Maybe I was looking for danger? Maybe I had no idea and was simply naïve? But I think I was genuinely looking for a mission to help me discover my true potential and identity.

The film started me thinking about what I wanted out of life and the direction I was going. So I researched the Royal Marines, made the decision to apply, and was offered a place after a long testing process. Around 14 months after that night at the cinema, I was starting day one of training, leaving the life I knew – and I never looked back.

New chapter

After intense training, I passed out of the Royal Marines as an original. To put into context how many originals pass out of a troop, let me give you some figures. In a troop of 60 original recruits, only around 3-8 get through to pass out as a Royal Marine Commando original. Many of those who leave the troop, do so voluntarily when they realise it's not for them. There are others who get injured along the journey, and some that just don't manage to meet the standard.

I also passed out as a diamond, which I was really proud of. It basically marks you as being one of the best performing recruits, and that you have shown potential leadership.

I was a nobody before I joined the Royal Marines. I was a guy lost in a world with no direction, I had one GCSE to my name, and was completely lost. Yet now I was passing out as a diamond, as a Royal Marine Commando, with the green lid on my head. I had worked hard for 32 weeks, and been pushed mentally, emotionally, and physically to reach that stage. I thought back to the advert that I had watched at the cinema, and to those two men wearing their green lids on my first day of training who had reassured me I was in the right place.

As I walked my family around the camp in my blues, we watched a new batch of recruits come in from the station, each one of them looking at us with envy. One of the guys nodded at me and I nodded back, knowing he probably needed some reassurance that he was in the right place.

It was the proudest day of my life so far.

Putting on the Big Boy pants

My first draft was to Plymouth, and I was lucky enough to join Juliet Company at 42 CDO, along with Ads, who had been one of my best mates through training.

An ex-professional footballer who was just good at everything, Ads had the better of me on the physical front, too. But that pushed me to raise my game through training, and we built up a great friendship over the 32 weeks.

The transition through training to operating at a unit took some getting used to, though. In training, you can't go out during the week because you have set routines to follow. It's a bit like prison (not that I've been!) – your life is limited, and you're restricted to camp.

At a unit, it's a totally different life. I remember going out for a meal the first night, and feeling as though I was going to be in the shit for leaving camp. It shows you how the routine had become drilled into my mindset; it had become part of my DNA.

When you're so used to a strict lifestyle for 32 weeks, it's very hard to relax. As recruits, we almost became wired, because the training team would be on you all of the time, ready to ambush you with a locker inspection or a thrashing. But now, there were just your mates, and a pass to go out when you wanted. We were able to wear our 'Big Boy' pants.

Career direction

In terms of your career, you have to move fast in a unit. You are told you have about a year there before being shipped up north somewhere onto a shit draft, or being selected to be a chef, driver, or signaller. And no one wanted those drafts! I remember my corporal in training (who was a sniper) always telling me that you have to make your own career, and can't sit around waiting for something to happen.

Some of the lads were leaving the Corps early because

they weren't feeling fulfilled any more. They wanted action, but not all of them were willing to work for what they wanted.

Ads, my mate from training, was living the dream. He was travelling around with the Royal Marine football team, doing what he did best.

My opportunity to take control of my career came in the way of a five-day sniper aptitude test, which decided if you were good enough to get onto the Royal Marine Snipers course. To my delight, I passed. I was thrilled, as I really hadn't known if I had it in me.

This course was recognised as the best sniper training in the Western world, with very high standards. It was designed to test soldiering skills, shooting ability, and mental aptitude. It's also where all the Special Forces soldiers would come to do their sniper training, which meant there was a real chance to gain some valuable experience from some of those lads.

In 2005, I passed the Royal Marine Sniper Course and returned to join 42 CDO recce troop. To be honest, this turned out to be the lowest point in my career. There were too many alpha males and shitty attitudes, and the environment was very cliquey, which wasn't for me.

Many of the guys thought they were better than the others, but I realise now that these lads were just young and emotionally immature. There were, however, some great corporals in the troop who kept them in order. And with hindsight, it was good experience for me to get through it and to understand that not all environments were going to be positive.

Deploying

In January 2006, I was called out of Norway training to deploy to Afghanistan as a small sniper team, to support J Company. J Company was one of the four companies that made a unit, and there were three units of Royal Marines that made the Brigade. A company consisted of around four troops, with support elements such as mortars, anti-tank, snipers, and recce troop.

Our main role was to protect the Royal Engineers, to patrol the area for Taliban movement, and to counter any threat while Camp Bastian was being built. For me, this was what it was all about, getting the opportunity to finally put into practice everything I had learned.

My heart, though, was split in two. Saying goodbye to my four-month-old daughter and my wife was gut-wrenching, and I kept wondering if it might be the last time I'd see them.

I suffered so much mentally at that time, but did the ego thing and never spoke about it, keeping my feelings inside. Every day was a struggle, and I missed home so much that at times I'd find myself walking away from the other guys and just crying. I'm a family man through and through, and when I was away from them, I couldn't help but feel vulnerable.

Those negative thoughts that you might not return home creep into your head during quiet periods. And although you can't afford to think like that, and to overthink the whole process, it was made even worse when I wrote my 'death letter' and left it on my bed every time we went out.

The death letter is given to your partner if something should happen to you. I wrote one for my then wife, and one for my little girl. Even though she was only a baby, I wrote a letter for when she was old enough to read it, and another one for her wedding day. This was an agonising process, but one that was advised. And every time we left the safety of the base, these letters would be left at the end of our beds.

We ended up spending five months in Afghanistan, and each day seemed like a week. Missing all those months of watching my little girl grow up was excruciatingly painful, and at times I questioned whether it was still what I wanted to do. I desperately loved the Corps, but my circumstances and priorities had changed from when I'd first joined, and I wanted to be a present father.

New openings

That same year I was drafted to CTCRM (Commando Training Centre Royal Marines) to help on the Royal Marine sniper course. This was a great opportunity for me, and I was so humbled to be helping on the course.

My role was to support the higher ranks and to organise the boys on the course. I felt well out of my comfort zone, and was very low on confidence about my abilities, mainly because the new team had such high pedigree. You could say I suffered from imposter syndrome.

However, during the two years I spent with that team, I learned so much, and I developed as a soldier and as a man. And a lot of the success I enjoyed after leaving the team can be attributed to the period of my life I spent working with these guys. They were incredibly supportive and patient with me, and I will always have fond memories of this chapter of my military life.

The hard work I put in during my spell there provided me with the opportunity to take a PTI (Physical Training Instructor) aptitude test. And this next part of the journey reshaped my direction and passion for the job. I was about to take on an absolute dream role in the forces.

My dream role

February 2008, I turned up for day one of the Royal Marine Physical Training Instructor Course, after finishing second out of 14 men in the aptitude test.

The course proved to be one of the most physically demanding in the world, and over a period of eight months I was thoroughly tested physically, mentally, and emotionally.

Initially, I struggled with that imposter syndrome mentality again. Many of the guys had more experience than me, and I had this overwhelming belief that I didn't deserve to be there, which really affected my confidence.

However, one comfort was that my mate from training, Ads, was on the course with me. All the way through training, we had talked about being a PTI and dreaming that one day we might get on this programme. So, to finally be there was the dream ticket for both of us.

The course was a bit of a nightmare for me at the start, as I had huge ITB (iliotibial band syndrome) pain in my right knee, which prevented me from doing any running for three weeks. At one point it looked as though I might even have to leave the course, which would have been a nightmare scenario.

Somehow, though, I managed to get through the pain, and made progress over an eight-month period. The guys I met on that course were brilliant, and as time went on, I felt less like an imposter and more like one of them.

This programme changed me in a multitude of ways. It showed what I was capable of, and again pushed me mentally and emotionally, constantly stretching my comfort zone to new levels in coaching, delivery, and physically. I found myself on a steep learning curve – and just loved the whole process.

I completed the course in September 2008. And apart from the birth of my children, I can still say to this day that it was the proudest moment of my life. I never thought I'd get to wear the illustrious white vest and cross clubs on my chest, and it was a real standout moment for me to be part of this club.

It had been a dream of mine from day one of joining the military. I remember seeing it in the brochure when I signed up, and saying that it was what I wanted to do. Finally, I had achieved it.

But my learning wasn't done there.

A step up in leadership

Step 2 was to attend the next JCC (junior command course), which is basically your promotion to corporal. This meant that if I was sent to war, I'd be in command of seven other men. So, it brought huge responsibility, which I loved.

The JCC course was brilliant. It was a case of going back to my roots in the sniper days, and demonstrating my skillset and leadership in the field.

During my days of being in recce troop, with their corporals and sergeant, and having been a part of the sniper training team, I had spent time around some of the most experienced and skilled soldiers the Royal Marines and Special Forces had to offer. And now I could put that experience and knowledge to good use.

I loved being in the field. I loved the organisation it brought to my life; it's what I had signed up to do. Putting the camouflage on my face, crawling around enemy positions, picking up intel, planning attacks – it was a childhood vision that I was now doing for real.

When I was a young kid, I used to run around the seafront, using a stick as a pretend gun and acting like I was a soldier. I even had little toy soldiers, and I would plan attacks on other toy soldiers. I had been obsessed with it as a kid. And now, here I was, training to be a leader, with real guns and scenarios, and doing this alongside some awesome guys.

I finished my Junior Command Course in December

2008, and was proud to finish fourth out of around 100 blokes. I would have had a chance at coming top, but I fucked up a navigational exercise, which brought my average right down. Actually, I've never told anyone before that I flunked one of the navigation exercises. I was too embarrassed, because my navigation was meant to be shit hot as a sniper. So, I imagine I'll get some shit for that now!

I wasn't dwelling on that blip, though. 2008 had been a huge year in my career. At the start of it, I was a Royal Marine trained rank; by the end of the year, I was a Physical Training Instructor (PTI) corporal in the Royal Marines. It was a title I was proud to have, and one I'd worked damn hard to achieve.

Curveball

I was now looking forward to some home time, and some consistent family life, as we now had two children. But how wrong I was.

I was tagged to be an ATI (adventure training instructor), which is a sub branch to being a PTI. You basically live the dream, teaching trained ranks on R&R how to climb, orientate up the mountains, kayak, and canoe. In the winter, you'd train them to ski.

I was offered the opportunity to go and learn to ski for four months in Germany, at the Navy Outdoor Centre, literally spending every day out on the slopes skiing. I was really torn, as I wanted to spend time at home after a year of being on courses, but it would have been frowned upon if I had said no. So off I went.

I had an incredible time, learned to ski like a boss, and I thoroughly embraced my new environment. The downside, though, was being away from home – again. The long absences were starting to take their toll on my personal life. I was missing out on the kids growing up, and I wasn't around to help my wife. She felt lonely and isolated, and I failed to see that at the time.

If I'm honest, I was becoming increasingly selfish in my ways, because it was starting to feel as though I was a single guy. I suppose it's only natural when you spend a huge amount of time by yourself, or travelling from one camp to another. It's one of the pitfalls of military life.

I found all the emotions so conflicting and confusing. In one way, I lived like a single guy, failing to be around the family environment enough and going from one place to the next. At other times, I'd be thrown back into family life, with all its responsibilities, and that can be hard for the brain to catch up. I was also too young and emotionally immature to deal with it all in the correct manner.

Finding my super power

In April 2009, I spent the next 12-18 months learning my trade as a PTI. I took four troops through training – three of which passed out of the gym at distinction level. When I took on the fourth troop, they were already five weeks into their journey and looked like being a disaster. But we managed to get them through with a pass in just four weeks.

This was one of the first times I recognised my 'super power', if you want to call it that. I believe everyone has one. It's just a case of finding it, or it finding you. That super power for me was getting the best out of people.

I wasn't the shouty type of coach or instructor. That side of me only came out occasionally – usually when the guys fucked me off too many times and I lost my patience, so I needed to recalibrate them. They might not have done anything wrong, but we'd mess them about a bit. It's all part of the process of character building for the recruits, creating the right state of mind. I'd call it a tactical thrashing.

I always believed to get the best out of a man you had to connect with him on an emotional and mental level, to understand what made him tick, what got the mind and body moving like an Elite Operator. Even back then, I used the term Elite Operator. Getting the individual to believe in their own ability and self-worth for the greater good of the troop was how you instilled an ethos of one in, all in. That belief and mindset tightened the bond of the troop. And the tighter the bond, the better the performance, the more confidence spread through the troop, and the more they believed in themselves to get through training.

I don't really know where my style of coaching came from. The training, for sure, provided me with the basics. But I believe that finishing my training was just the start of a new chapter; it was time to fill the blank book. And that blank book is how you build your legacy, with your thoughts, approaches, decisions, implementations, and failures. You add your identity into that troop with your passion, your standards, and your mindset.

I like to think that I left a lasting legacy with those men that I trained between 2009-2010. And I still take great pride in having developed hundreds of men from civilians into trained Royal Marine Commandos, ready for service.

At my leaving do, one thing that stood out for me was when the chief did his piece on me, which was the tradition in the PTI branch. He said, 'I don't know what he does, but he seems to get the absolute best out of the men he works with.'

I've never forgotten those words. They've always stuck with me, and been the ethos for building my career as a coach.

Next chapter

In 2010, I was offered a place on the first ever Royal Navy ATI (Adventure Training Instructor) course. This was another eight-month course, but this time it was in Llanrwst, North Wales.

By that stage, the family had moved back home to East Sussex. We had agreed that we didn't want to up sticks every time I was drafted or sent away, and my then wife needed support with the kids as they started primary school.

It was about an eight-hour round trip from East Sussex to Llanrwst, so trips home were few and far between, which was gutting. The course itself, though, was one of my favourite times in the military. Learning every day to kayak, canoe, climb, mountaineer, how could it not be? There were two other lads on the course – Mags and Gareth, two Navy boys. They were absolutely sound, and I'll always have very fond memories of our time together there.

The whole experience pushed me in new ways, including coaching styles, and scary experiences like kayaking down grade four rivers and climbing multi-pitch rock faces (I was no longer afraid of heights).

I found the whole experience allowed me to drop my ego and truly connect with myself. I came out of that course a much better person, and it massively helped in the progression of my career and my life.

Next stop – and what would prove to be my last – was at Talybont, South Wales, where I joined a Royal Navy Outdoor Centre to teach Royal Navy recruits and officers valuable leadership skills. I was able to walk the hills of Brecon regularly and to kayak once a week in the most beautiful lakes, so it was a great posting. And the guys who worked there were great fun to be around.

I had worked very hard to reach that position, and had faced a lot of tough times and adversity. But by that stage I could honestly say I had one of the best careers ahead of me in the military.

So it may surprise you to learn that I can't tell you the exact moment when I started to think about leaving. It could have been watching my kids cry their eyes out every Sunday night when I said goodbye for another week.

It could have been the fact that I missed too many school performances or sports days.

It could have been the fact that I just didn't want to be away from them for a long period of time again.

But I just couldn't get my head around the fact that something didn't sit right any more, and I felt totally conflicted. I had the job of my dreams, but I just wasn't happy or fulfilled any more.

The deciding factor

I honestly believe that if the opportunity to leave had not come about, I would never have quit the military, and today I'd be a Sergeant Major in an office somewhere, with six years left to serve… and still being a weekend dad.

However, the opportunity *did* present itself, with a position to teach outdoor education at a local authority establishment. And, on paper, it looked like the perfect role for me.

I toyed for ages about whether or not to complete the application form. Was I really going to leave this amazing job that I had worked so hard for, and when I had a great career ahead of me?

In short, the answer was YES. The desire to be a full-time father outweighed my career goals, and I have never truly regretted that choice. There may have been some occasions when I did, but they were just a reaction to the bad days.

I was interviewed for the job, and offered it right there and then. Shit just got real! A bit of me had been hoping that they'd give it to someone else, so that I didn't have to make the decision to leave.

When you resign from the military, you have to give one year's notice. I was offered the job in April 2011, and the job started in September 2011, so I had some strings to try and pull to get early release.

I hounded the officer in charge, and also my Major, and I massively appreciated that my boss was backing me all the way for early release. But when it finally came through, I remember feeling a wave of anxiety like never before. I suddenly felt incredibly vulnerable, and I was overcome by a whole host of emotions. Was I making the right decision? Fear set in like never before, and so did the overthinking. I guess I had secretly been hoping that my early release would not be approved.

On my last day, I packed up and said my goodbyes, then got in the car. But for the majority of the four-hour drive home, I wept uncontrollably, on and off, and kept questioning my decision.

Was this going to work out? Was I going to be okay? My whole military life flashed in front of my eyes – all the good and bad times, all the people I'd met, the career I had built. It was all about to become history, and just a memory.

The new job

Although it was a massive step, I genuinely had no idea the U-turn my life was about to take. In some ways, I realise now that I was extremely naïve to think that I could leave the military on a Friday and walk straight into a new life and new job on the Monday.

My job title was Teacher of Outdoor Education and Public Services, but I had no idea what I was doing. None. And I really mean that. The 16-19-year-old students saw me coming a mile away, and they completely tested the boundaries.

Some of these youngsters had huge potential, but most were ungrateful, entitled kids who had no idea of the opportunity they had in front of them. And I hated teaching them.

The men and women I had trained in the Navy and Royal Marines had been highly motivated and receptive to knowledge and experience so that they could learn and become the best version of themselves. In the military, students respected the rank, and the experience. They had discipline and focus.

These kids, on the other hand, had their mobile phones, and were only worried about where the next party was. They were immature, poorly prepared for this educational establishment, and just didn't want to learn.

However, I put my heart and soul into bettering them, instilling discipline, forward thinking, and self-awareness. But while there were some good students who I loved mentoring, most were just not interested. And getting work from them was like getting blood from a stone.

My short experience in education taught me a couple of things.

In my view, most senior management don't give a shit about the kids or the teachers. It's a money-making business, and is about putting bums on seats. I get it; it's a corporate world. And if you are not in line with that thinking, your face doesn't fit and you are out of there.

In my opinion, there are so many gaps in the education system that it's unreal. Where's all the mental health training? The financial awareness training? Where's the discipline? The standards? The values? I could write a book just on this subject alone.

Needless to say, I did not enjoy my time teaching there, and to top it all off, I was fighting a personal battle in my own head.

Sliding doors

That trauma was a severe identity crisis. I was still Sergeant James Boardman, but teaching in a civilian educational establishment. And the two just didn't match up!

I knew within four weeks that I didn't belong in the civilian world. I hated it... like, really *hated* it. So, after a month out of the military, I spoke to my old boss and he encouraged me to return. I spoke to my wife, and she supported me going back to the military. After a great deal of soul-searching, I walked back into the career's office on Saturday, October 15, to begin the process of reenlistment. And I just felt so relieved.

I signed for all my papers to be released, and was buzzing at the prospect of being able to join back up before

Christmas. In all honesty, I felt guilty that I hadn't made more of an effort to stay and be around my family, but my mind was crumbling, and I felt I was letting everyone down with the way I was struggling with everything.

I knew that I had to put myself first so that I could be the best for them. I was no good to them with my current state of mind, so I determined that I would be the greatest dad at weekends and on holidays, or whenever I could.

November came and went, and I heard nothing from the career's office. And when I phoned up to speak to the officer who was handling my application, I was told he had left at the start of November, and nobody knew anything about my case. I couldn't believe it.

This has to have been one of those sliding door moments and my life could have taken another dramatic U-turn at the end of 2011 with me returning to the military.

When I was asked to return to organise the paperwork and get the process underway, I agreed. But I never showed up. I never got a follow-up call either, and I never heard from my previous boss. In my mind, this was the universe's way of telling me that this wasn't my path any more, that my journey belonged out of the military, and somehow I had to rediscover myself to make my life work on the outside.

Becoming a car crash

It became apparent in that first six months of being out of the military that something wasn't right with me, inside me. In my head, I wasn't right. I was acting up, I was out of character, aggressive, drinking, and highly anxious.

I had taken a £12k-a-year pay cut by becoming a civilian, and that instantly created a massive amount of pressure for the family. We were on the bones of our arse, and I felt absolutely useless.

I started running a part-time fitness bootcamp just two days a week – Saturday mornings and Wednesday evenings – to bring in a little extra cash. But I'd never visualised that I'd feel so helpless, as if I was letting my family down by having no money or security, and becoming so distant. I also never expected it would create the trouble it did.

By the end of 2012, I was divorced. This was no one else's fault, other than mine, and I accept full responsibility for the fact that I allowed the relationship to fail. I let down my wife and kids at the time, and I felt we were on different paths, on top of the issues I had created.

When you join the military, you tend to lose some of your identity, of who you used to be. The truth is that I had gone through such a character change during my served time that when I left the military, I had no idea who I was any more.

I was an empty shell walking around. I was a fraction of the Sgt James Boardman that I knew. I was unrecognisable, and I wasn't reaching out to anybody for help because I was too embarrassed and ashamed, or maybe too ego-driven to admit there was an issue.

I made the decision to break away from the family because I felt I had created too much trouble and heartbreak, and couldn't handle the repercussions of my errors. I didn't know how to cope with it. Mentally, I was spiralling out of control, heading deeper into dead ground, burying myself a little more each day.

After the divorce, I was financially on the edge. Utterly broke, I was drinking, I wasn't training, I was a car crash. And the whole time I was still struggling to figure out what the hell I was doing working at the educational establishment. Somehow, though, I managed to keep my mask on and to hide all this inner conflict from everyone around me.

Eventually, it reached the stage where I didn't really see a future for myself. I couldn't leave my job because I would lose the house, so I felt totally trapped. It was like wearing a straitjacket; there was just no movement.

On top of that, I felt I was failing as a father, and had already failed as a husband, and a man (whatever that meant). There was so much uncertainty in my life that I didn't know how to control the overwhelming anxiety and conflict that dominated my every thought.

And that is what led me to be sitting on the bed that night, as I strongly contemplated taking my own life.

I couldn't stop crying. I kept telling myself I'd fucked my life up. I'd had everything in the military, but now I had nothing through no fault of my own. I felt like I was a no one. What was the point of being there? I was ready to give up.

The darkest point

I had placed a large number of pills out on the bed alongside a large bottle of whisky, and I was in such a state I was prepared to neck the lot. I didn't know if it would kill me, but I was willing to give it a shot in the hope that it would. I had every intention of overdosing.

As everything swirled around in my head, I looked up at the picture of my two gorgeous kids and I thought what a let-down I'd been to them. I had moved home to be an inspiration and role model to them, but now look at me!

I genuinely can't really explain to you what made me get up off the floor right then and go for a run. But looking at that photograph gave me a moment of clarity and the inspiration to move away from the idea of ending my life.

It was similar to the feeling I'd had when I didn't reapply for the military. The best way to describe it is just a gut instinct that connects to your brain and for a split second makes total sense. It's like being in the eye of a storm, and everything becomes still just long enough to see things clearly and act.

The run

I got up… and I ran and walked for three solid hours. I just wanted to get out of the house, and had initially planned to go out for about 30 minutes or so. On that run, I cried, laughed, put things into perspective, and reflected. I thought about the man I had become in the Royal Marines, and the man I had failed to be when I left the Royal Marines.

Somehow, that run cleared the storm in my mind, and when I finally returned, I poured the whisky down the drain and put the tablets away.

Something changed in me that night. I found qualities and strength that I had gained during my career as a Royal Marine, but hadn't unearthed in a long time. I can only put it down to that run clearing my mind, balancing the chemicals in my brain, and allowing me to fall back into that strong identity of Sgt James Boardman.

I found a spark inside me to get a grip and take some control of my life again. I had fallen so far that I knew I faced a long and difficult journey. But that glimmer of light at the end of the tunnel after the run was enough to wake me up.

When it rains, it pours

Some of you that already follow me will know this as the 1% win. I found a shred of purpose, something to live for, and that was my two children, Angelina and Bailey.

No one knew what I was going through or what I had experienced that night. NO ONE! But just as that tiny spark was lit inside me, it was about to be challenged – and I didn't even see it coming.

It was deemed that my part-time job of taking fitness classes was affecting my main job as a teacher, and I found myself suspended from work. This was despite my high observations in audit scores, and despite the grades I had got out of the kids. This was all overlooked.

What they really meant was that they were looking for a scapegoat to save money, and I was that goat. They had no idea what I had sacrificed to take that job or what I was going through at the time, and I suspect they wouldn't have cared. It's a business; it's about results, not people!

The whole procedure lasted four weeks, but luckily I was a member of a union that helped me with the disciplinary board. My case worker was called Anna, and she was the union's Sgt Major, and as cutthroat as me.

It was my first experience of having to deal with corporate monkeys (the senior management team), and it all came around at the same time as I was desperately struggling to keep my wits about me with financial worries, my mental well-being, and the aftermath of divorce.

Even after a few good weeks of building momentum, I was still at breaking point and the employment situation felt like a real punch in the face. Although they had nothing on me whatsoever, it was clear on my second interview with the Human Resources team that, despite there being no wrongdoing on my part, I couldn't stay in the job.

The relationship between employee and employer had broken down, and I couldn't work for a management team that I felt lacked integrity. I had learned the hard way how they treated their staff, so when I was offered a settlement, I took it.

When I look back at this situation, I now realise that

this was another example of the universe's way of guiding me to a much bigger and better future. Before I had been suspended, I had been looking at the shit effort a student had displayed in his assessment, and thought to myself, *This can't be it for me for the next 30 years, surely? This is not what I'm built for.*

But it's funny how you can be directed to the next chapter of your life. I often look back at how I handled that whole experience, and realise that it gave me great leverage to continue building myself up once again. It gave me the fire to go all-in on *me*, and to take control of my life again.

The new identity

Initially, I was paralysed by fear that I was going to be homeless because I no longer had any regular income to pay for the mortgage. However, I had a little money from the settlement, and along with some money I borrowed from my mum, I had enough to survive on for about four months.

I felt extremely liberated after leaving the toxic environment of the educational establishment. I had learnt some tough lessons and witnessed some unbelievably poor management, particularly how not to treat your staff and other human beings. So, I looked at this as just another learning curve to add to my experience. Learn, Grow, Repeat, right?

But what was next? The world was my oyster and I

could do anything I wanted. So, I decided I was going to go all-in on my bootcamp. Yet I had no idea how to run a business; I imagine any 16-year-old studying business for GCSE would know more.

I went for it anyway. When I left the job, my outgoings were £2500, and my income from the side hustle was around £400. That meant my survival pot was going to run out fast, so I had to find ways to save money. From then on, I only ever put the heating on when the kids came around, and I lived off Tesco value beans, bread, and teabags, so my outgoings were minimal. That brought down my monthly outgoings and relieved the financial stress slightly. But even then, I was still financially vulnerable.

Switching identities

At that point in my life, I was leaving behind two identities. First, I had to come to terms with the fact that I was no longer a Royal Marine PTI. I wasn't Sgt James Boardman any more, and I had to stop pretending I was still him in this current chapter of my life. It wasn't allowing me to move on; a bit like an ex that stays inside your head.

Second, I had to mentally close the educational establishment chapter. It had been my stepping stone out of the military and, despite my unhappy experience there, I had met some great fellow teachers and students. And I had learned a lot about what I *didn't* want in life.

Today, I sometimes find it hard to believe that I ever

worked there, as it was such a blip in time. But I was happy to leave it behind, having learnt a lot about myself.

My new identity came in the form of entrepreneurship, and Bodyshock Fitness was the name I came up with for my company. I had no idea how it would play out, but I rolled my sleeves up and put the effort in. This was a case of *I MUST* make this work, not *I should* make this work.

I spent every waking moment building the company and learning about business – the software required, the funnels needed, the essential strategies and models to be successful. I listened to podcasts, I read books, I lived on YouTube watching videos on how to run a business. I gave away free personal training sessions to build my brand and reputation, and was working 16-hour days.

I had gone from being an anxious, scared man, suffering from depression and a victim mentality, to a businessman that was on a mission, and things were moving fast. The process was helping me to grow and learn at a rapid rate, and as my work ethic was second to none, I saw a gap in the market where my competitors had allowed complacency to creep in.

I had always been taught to outwork the competition, and that's what I did. No one saw me coming, everyone underestimated me, and no amount of shit chat about me from competitors was going to stop me.

Bodyshock Fitness helped me create a new identity. It gave me a thirst for life and knowledge, and my engine was on fire. It's hard to believe that just six months previously, I had been staring down the barrel of a bottle of whisky and some tablets.

Now, I woke up most mornings with drive, passion, and desire. I had made new friends, I had renewed confidence, I even had enough money to stop eating supermarket brand foods and to put the heating on when it was needed. The first time I was able to take the kids out to eat at a restaurant will always be a special memory for me.

I won't lie, though. I still struggled mentally and emotionally. I still doubted myself, and fought the demons every now and then. My self-worth was still low. But I had moved forward 1% a day, with the sole purpose of creating a better future for me and the kids.

Building momentum

During the early years of Bodyshock, my partner (now my wife!) and I officially got together. At first, I was dubious whether I wanted another relationship, but Jem was a one-in-a-million. She helped me become a much better man, and has continued to do so throughout our time together. She is my best mate in the world, and I'm super proud of the mum she has become.

In the first year of business by myself, the company had taken £100k. That's not a brag, it's a fucking achievement, going from the bones of my arse to building this business. I couldn't believe it.

I put everything into Bodyshock because I had no choice but to go all-in. I used all the qualities and experience I had gained in the military to create my masterpiece, helping thousands of people become fit and strong along the way. This was a huge achievement for me, and all of those small wins added up over time.

When I reviewed my first year in business, I took a moment to think back to when I had been facing the prospect of losing my house and possibly ending my life. Now I had this new lease of life, where I almost lived life on my terms, helping people to achieve their own success. And I was making an impact – something I have always thrived on.

I thought back to my chief's words when I was leaving the Royal Marines: 'I don't know what he does, but he seems to get the absolute best out of the people he works with.'

I had gone through a tumultuous four-year cycle, but I was back in a place doing what I did best: getting the best out of those wanting to be their best.

The transition

On 18th April 2017, Alba was born – the latest addition to my beautiful family. I needed her as much as she needed me, as I was hitting a stage in my life where I felt I needed to shift focus.

Bodyshock Fitness had taught me so much, but I was now starting to feel like an employee in my own business and it was making me miserable.

The business was dominating me because I was obliged

to be at the classes and to take them. And although I did hire some incredible staff to help me, I think it was too late. By that stage I was falling out of love with the business.

Having Alba made me realise that I wasn't living life on my terms any more. Money wasn't the drive; freedom was. So, in 2017 I started the early transition phase of doing what I actually wanted to do.

It had taken me many years to realise what my new mission was, and that was to help men become Elite Operators in life again. I wanted to get the absolute best out of those men who wanted to get the best out of themselves. Having gone through what I did, I wanted to use my experience to help these guys take control of the reins once again, and make sense of where they were in their lives.

But I wanted this to be an online business. I had missed so much of my first two children's lives by being away with the military, and I didn't want the same scenario with Alba. Working every night and morning, missing key time with her, was hard to do.

I also wanted the freedom to be able to be there for my older two, whenever they wanted to hang out with me. So running an online business was the obvious way to go.

I created and founded The Dad Coach, wrote my first book *It's a State of Mind,* and went all-in. It was like starting Bodyshock Fitness again, but I had no clue what I was doing as I hadn't worked online before. So I learned. I put the work in again to learn how to make an online business a success.

I studied, I figured out, I got down and dirty again, even

renting an office and hiring Luisa to help me with admin. She had been one of my instructors for Bodyshock Fitness, and is an absolute rock for me in the business.

Where we are now?

Fast forward three years, and we've rebranded to The Man Coach, we've sold over 15,000 copies of *It's a State of Mind*, we've helped over 10,000 men in our FREE 5-Day Challenge, we've helped thousands of men on our 28-Day Man-Made Project, and are helping hundreds of guys daily in our Mastermind.

And we're not stopping there!

We are going to be taking on the world, and helping men in other continents – guys who are battling to keep their heads above water. The fire is burning, and we have a mission to complete.

At this point, I want to put some context on 'WE'. We is my core team of Jon, Mary Anne, and Mikey B, along with all my ambassadors – Gary P, Gary E, Jez, Paul, and Spencer. All of these guys were once clients who have come through my system and become part of the journey for many of the men now coming through our world.

External members of my team are my mentor, marketing expert, and best mate Phil, and then there's Cathy, Jonny, Mike, and the members in Phil's Mastermind, who all help and contribute to the running of my business and are new friends of mine.

And we are about to start a brand new phase of the mission, helping entrepreneurs to become the asset of their business. It again means going through the pains of a start-up, but it's exciting and it's worth it.

To add to all that, in 2022, I'm marrying my amazing partner Jem.

I can now honestly say I'm starting to live life on my own terms, working with who I want to, and feeling mentally and emotionally stronger. I'm rich in time, and that's the only 'rich' I need in my life.

Undoubtedly, the last eight years have been a roller coaster. But I wanted to share the progress of the business and my family because I want you to see that life *can* be better, that good things *can* happen, even during some of the hardest periods of your life.

In some respects, I want to be that vision for you – just like those two Royal Marines I saw on day one of my training.

It's never too late to start focusing on yourself, and making things better. If I had sat around feeling sorry for myself in a world of self-pity and victim mentality, I wouldn't be where I am today. I am here now purely because of the dedication I showed myself in changing my state of mind and fighting for my life – showing the fuck up.

Whenever I feel like not showing up, I go back to that dark place, as that is the stark alternative. Do I want that life? Hell, no, FUCK THAT! I'm here to make the most of every second I have, to leave a legacy of some sort, both personally and professionally.

I don't have time to feel sorry for myself, or turn my issues into depression; there's no time for that any more. We have limited time to make our mark on the world.

When you are on a mission, you focus on the mission like an Elite Operator patrolling through life. And I want to help you do that! But are you ready to put in the work?

You only have to follow these two rules:

1) To show the fuck up, 1% a day
2) To meet me halfway every day

Those are my only rules, and if you follow them you will win; you can't lose.

I'm happy to help you figure it all out and show you how to become an Elite Operator, but there can be no shortcuts or room for excuses.

I want this book to help you develop that mental edge required to keep showing up, to understanding yourself better, to be able to answer your own questions.

I won't lie – there's a lot to take in. And if you try to change it all at once, it will become too much. So you need to take things one step at a time, constantly checking in on your alter ego, facing yourself in the mirror and asking if your standard is high enough to live the life you're after.

3

What Is an Elite Operator?

Visualising your Elite Operator

When you read the phrase Elite Operator, what does that mean to you? You might have an image in your mind, but what does it stand for? How does it help you? What does it look like to you?

I want to give you my vision as an example, as an introduction to what it represents to me and how it will help you to raise your standards and level of thinking.

The Elite Operator is an alter ego that fears no situation, no environment, no one. When he operates, he does so clinically, meticulously, with clear focus and an overwhelming desire to achieve the mission.

When he's on a mission, he's focused purely on that mission, without distraction, confusion, or complication. He's not deterred by negativity, toxic environments, or adversity. He's resilient and robust enough to stay focused purely on the mission.

He's consistent in his drills and repetition to perform

daily tasks that align with his mission. He's in control of his time, energy, and emotions, to be as effective as possible in his day-to-day activities. He has total clarity on the mission and what's required to achieve it.

An Elite Operator doesn't waste time becoming frustrated about the things he can't control. He dominates what he *can* control and executes with precision whatever is in his circle of influence.

He lives by his most valued rules that guide him to follow specific habits, routines, and structure. The development of his structure provides his growth, education, and understanding of how to become more efficient and resilient in day-to-day life.

The Elite Operator is fearless; he doesn't spend time wallowing in self-pity, and he doesn't fuel a victim mentality. He doesn't surround himself with others who bring him down, or try to hold him back, or even tell him what he should be doing.

He doesn't run away when things get hard and the going gets tough. He won't bury his head in the sand, because that would blind him from his mission and deter him from seeing the facts of the current situation, which would act as a barrier to restrict his progress in life. He doesn't make excuses as to why he can't show up; he simply finds a way to be there.

The Elite Operator mindset, though, takes time to create and grow. It's a long play. Repetition of action, showing up, and hard work all help to create the alter ego that gives you the inner mental and emotional strength and awareness to stay ahead in life.

Setting the standard for yourself

Let me ask you: is there any part of you that is an Elite Operator? A standard that you set yourself to meet every day? Values and principles that you live by? A mindset that is strong enough to resist the temptations and distractions of the world?

I'm talking about a standard that will always keep you on the edge of your comfort zone, one that will guide you to achieving the best version of yourself – not just for you, but for those around you. If you don't have anything like this in place, it's probably fair to say you're most likely falling below the standard required to be where you want to be in life.

Have you been accepting a 'just getting by' standard, that really doesn't offer you the results you so desperately want? Have you been falling down on the standards you set yourself, or lowering them? Setting low standards for yourself tends to affect your confidence and self-worth, and – more worryingly –your health, relationships, and your future.

The crucial thing you have to understand is that your Elite Operator (alter ego) will follow you everywhere. It will be your subconscious, and will keep you accountable for every action that you take – or don't take – because you can't hide from your own reflection forever!

If you like, the Elite Operator is your self-awareness. So, the more that you can connect with your alter ego, the more you challenge yourself in your day-to-day life and the actions you take. That voice in your head becomes a conversation with your Elite Operator, not with the chimp.

Raising your awareness

In this book, I want to teach you how to build and grow this state of mind. And I'm going to deliver some harsh truths that I've witnessed from working with thousands of men since my first book was published three years ago. And I'll do it so that I can help you win.

It will save your marriage, your relationship with your kids, your job, and most importantly YOU! If you listen and act.

More than likely, you need some form of guidance in your life in one way or another. Some people will need more guidance than others before they crash and burn. Others just need to sharpen the sword. So, take from the book what *you* need, and implement it as best you can to help get you to the place you want to be.

Let's start by dropping the ego! You might be feeling a bit lost in life, or struggling to figure out who you are at the minute. Maybe you have no direction.

It doesn't matter whether you desperately need help or are just a little lost and curious. There's scope to raise your game whatever level you're at.

Avoiding the truth

Stop reading the book for a few minutes, go to the mirror, and look at yourself for two minutes! Take a look in the mirror right now and say out loud, 'I need this.' Then ask yourself: Am I living my life or just existing in it? Am I growing in life or constantly crashing? Am I happy in life or am I miserable?

It's time to answer some really tough questions of yourself, so you have to open up and be totally honest. No one likes hearing or accepting the truth; it can be upsetting and trigger all sorts of emotions, which is why so many of us avoid it.

But hiding from the truth is like putting yourself in a straitjacket, or walking around with a ball and chain. It restricts your progress and just holds you back.

Let's be blunt. Isn't it time you snapped the fuck out of your self-pity bubble and the victim mentality about how the world is against you, how it's everyone else's fault but yours, and start regaining some control of your life and accepting some responsibilities?

You are an Elite Operator in the making.

Many people will not get through this; it's too difficult for them to make the breakthrough. But you, my man, you can get through it. You have just empowered the Elite Operator inside of you by facing your truth, by making the decision to be in control of your life again, to be in charge of your own decisions again, to allow yourself to be the ultimate version of YOU once more. That feeling of control will empower you and allow the walls to stop closing in.

Every decision you make, I want you to confer with your Elite Operator. Not your chimp. Your chimp has been in control for too long, so it's time to implement a new approach to life. And having that strong wingman, that Elite Operator, will only strengthen your state of mind.

4

The 1% Rule

I want to explain this mentality to you. It's about understanding your own expectations versus your own level of conditioning, based on where you are today.

I regularly participate in BJJ (Brazilian Jiu Jitsu), so I am going to use this sport and its grading system as an analogy.

Imagine yourself as a BJJ white belt – the colour of belt for a beginner, someone at the start of their journey. You've been practising BJJ for eight weeks, and in that time you've grown in confidence and are starting to demand more from yourself.

In training one day, you start rolling (grappling) with a purple belt. To give some context, a purple belt is someone that will have anywhere between six and 12 years of experience, compared to your eight weeks. So, the chances are that you are going to be both out-skilled and out-performed, based on your experience and conditioning.

When you leave the club after that morning's training, you've been well beaten. But that is a common part of the process, and you can only get better by embracing the learn, grow, repeat process. You learn by being out-skilled and losing; you grow by learning not to make the same mistakes again; you gain valuable experience, and repeat the process. Eventually, your conditioning improves, as does your skillset, standards, and mindset. But...

This is where you start piling on the personal pressure, by having expectations of yourself that don't meet your current conditioning, mentally, emotionally, and physically. It almost becomes an ego thing, if you like.

So, what happens when this scenario plays out? What do you say to yourself? You go back to that child mentality in the playground and say, 'I'm shit at this!' or 'What's the point? This is crap.' You become angry, frustrated, and emotional. You start feeling sorry for yourself as a by-product of the deficit between your expectations and level of conditioning. Maybe you start to blame everyone else for your reaction, but remember it's only you that has misplaced the level of expectation you have on yourself.

I often see this scenario when it comes to nutrition and training programmes. I hear, 'This diet plan isn't working.' Or 'I'm not losing any weight on this plan.' Sound familiar?

The reality is that you aren't tracking your calories properly, or you aren't really following the programme, and/or you haven't given it enough time and attention and put in the required work.

You'll argue that you have. But the reality is that you haven't tracked everything, and that you haven't been patient or shown up to make the programme work. Instead, you've built up an expectation and it hasn't happened quickly enough for you. Or you've prioritised work commitments, or didn't manage your time correctly, so you've bailed and just not shown up.

Going back to the original example of BJJ training, you haven't been training long enough to keep up with the purple belt, so you bail. And, once again, the process and consistency of change is disrupted.

Take a moment to think of where and when something like this has happened in your life. Where have you set the expectations too high for the actual level of conditioning you were at? What were the consequences, the emotions, the reactions, the decisions you made? Be honest with yourself. Opening up to mistakes or misplaced priorities is a great learning experience and really raises your levels of self-awareness.

EXAMPLE:

I started playing football again recently at the age of 42, after seven years out of the sport, and I believed I could keep up with any of the lads. As a result of thinking I was still as fit and sharp as I had been seven years before, I injured myself constantly. My hamstrings were regularly straining, my calf was under pressure, I wasn't as sharp on the ball, and my passing range was shot to pieces. I felt pretty frustrated at not being the player I used to be, and becoming injured all the time. My expectations were unrealistic for my levels of condition, both physically and mentally. So, I've since decided to only be available as a sub for the last 20 minutes of the game, which is a much more realistic expectation for me to reach.

Getting this right?

Being honest with yourself and achieving balance is so important here. There's a gap in the deficit between what you are capable of and what your expectations are, so you need to be able to equal this out.

I'll use running as an example to make sense of this process. Let's say you are a beginner runner, which means understanding that a 10k run is most likely out of your reach right now. The thought of running six miles makes you feel anxious and nervous, but that's okay; it's nothing to be embarrassed about. You're a beginner, so accepting your limitations at this point in time is the honesty part. Sure, you might have run once upon a time, but it was a long while ago, so you are going to have to go back to the beginners' stage and build up. You'll have to drop that ego and accept where you are!

Managing those expectations early

When you were a baby, you obviously couldn't walk. It was something you had to learn to do. But we all eventually get there with persistence, pushy parents, and that will to keep going. Back then, when we were just starting out on our first steps, we didn't suffer from self-doubt or overthinking.

When it comes to building yourself up now, I need you to almost go back to having that baby brain. We need to eradicate your self-doubt and overthinking, and just take action without thinking.

Let's say your limit as a beginner runner is maybe 2-4k at the moment – maybe even walk/run, but it's manageable. When you complete each run, it gives you a feeling of satisfaction that you've achieved a milestone and a start point.

As time progresses, and the weeks turn into months, you become more conditioned physically, mentally, and emotionally – similar to a baby transitioning from crawling to walking. It also means your expectations rise. You've built up confidence in what you can achieve, and you've stretched your limitations.

Enter overthinking and self-doubt…

One of the issues you'll face throughout this process is comparing yourself and your current level of conditioning to someone else. You'll use statements like, 'It's not as good as your 100-miler' and 'It was a pretty slow run' or 'You're all better runners than me.'

But when in your mind does good become good enough? And why are you underselling your own achievements? It's *your* fucking achievement, dude. You earned it.

You have to stop caring about what anyone else is doing. Why are you judging yourself against others? You are trying to be the best version of yourself, not the best version of anyone else. Everyone and every situation is different – your fitness levels at the time, your age, what you've gone through, genetics, your life responsibilities, your history of running. That's why it's important not to compare yourself to others.

That mindset becomes a wall to stop you progressing further with your development. You micro-fail yourself, and the positivity you should be experiencing becomes clouded by thoughts of 'It's not good enough'. You feel that your performance or result isn't as good as what others are doing, so it's no good at all. But do you know how mad that sounds? Say it out loud. Are you honestly saying it's not good enough because you don't meet the standards of someone else?

Please give yourself a virtual slap around the face, and wake yourself the fuck up.

This is *your* chapter, *your* journey, *your* process, *your* progression. Don't look for progression based on others' achievements. Base your progression on your own standards, and allow yourself the wins, the pat on the back, the milestone. Don't find the flaws in the wins!

Self-limiting beliefs

When you were at school, no doubt there was one particular girl that was so hot to you. You'd secretly stare at her and imagine that she'd say 'Yes' if you asked her out. There's always that one girl – or maybe that's just me. Anyway…

That girl in my year was Vicky. When she spoke to me, I melted and said something ridiculous that made me look like a cock. I wasn't very confident around girls I liked back then, and considered myself ugly. That's what I told myself, so that's what I believed.

I had such a crush on her, and it was written all over my face. I would constantly visualise asking her out and us going on a date. I can't believe I'm admitting this now, but I'd actually practise in the mirror at home! I thought that if she was my girlfriend, I'd be the happiest 14-year-old alive.

Do you know why she was never my girlfriend? Why we never got to go on a date, or hang out at the weekend?

Unless you try, you won't know

It wasn't because she said, 'No.' It was because I didn't think I was good enough to ask her out. I thought I was ugly, I wasn't a cool kid, I was bullied through school. So why would she go out with me? I didn't even try. How sad is that?

I'll never know what she would have said, and that's a pretty sad part of my childhood. She signed my school shirt 'I hope to see you again' along with kisses. But I never did see her again.

Imagine if you collected in a sack all of the things you didn't do in your life due to your internal self-limiting beliefs, or because of fear. The races you didn't run, the girls you never asked out, the jobs you never applied for, the courses you never signed up to.

If you hadn't had those self-limiting beliefs, what would you have achieved? What would be different? Would you feel more fulfilled and happier, maybe more accomplished?

Here's a scenario played out

If I apply for this job, what if I don't like it and I'm stuck there? What if I get found out? I don't want to feel like an imposter.

The job could bring you more family time, as it is based closer to home, and it has more opportunities in terms of growth and promotion. On the other hand, I'm really comfortable where I am, and I don't want to be the weak link in a new team.

Anxiety, anxiety, anxiety, overthink, overthink, overthink.

You've just created your own self-limiting beliefs, and blocked yourself from taking up a possibly amazing opportunity. And that in a nutshell is your mind when it comes to doing anything. You talk yourself out of nearly everything, thinking you aren't good enough. You're overthinking the process and are weighed down by fear.

Leap of faith

Sometimes you just have to take a leap of faith and say, 'Fu*k it, let's see what happens.' If you are always thinking the worst-case scenario, how will you ever move forward? Part of learning and growing is stepping into the unknown and accepting that failure is part of the process. But if you don't try, you'll never know!

It's time to take a good, long, hard look in the mirror, stop beating yourself up, stop overthinking, and stop setting the bar too fucking high too soon.

You can't fool me; I've taken every step you have. I've faced the black clouds, and I've dealt with the demons and the voices of uncertainty that hold you back from being where you want to be.

Now it's time to put on the Elite Operator hat and start smashing down any walls that try to get in the way of my mission.

In this book I'm going to help you establish the Elite Operator mentality to do just that, so that you can focus on your mission.

Are you with me?

Are you committed?

Have you got your game face on?

We've looked at the reality of your situation, and I've given you a brief description of who I am. I've introduced you to the Elite Operator mindset, and discussed how your expectations can grind you to a halt without accepting your current levels of conditioning.

So, are you now ready to create your mission – the most important phase of creating the new version of you? This will be your map, your North Star, your compass, your blueprint, your purpose. It's the reason you'll show up, even when you don't feel like it.

5

Expectations Vs Current Conditioning

Using your alter ego

It's important to understand what I mean visually and emotionally when I say 'Remember the Mission'. If you are going to embrace this ethos, I want to give some context behind the words to help you understand this process.

You may have seen in films, pictures, or books, images of Special Forces soldiers all kitted up, looking professional and ready for action. My personal vision of the Elite Operator is that image of the Special Forces soldier ready to go into battle – pretty much like I was before going on patrol in Afghanistan.

You don't have to have been in the military to have this vision. There are numerous films in which you see these character types. As explained in the earlier chapters, it's just an example; an image or vision which my alter ego can really leverage on when I step up each day.

When I operate in my day-to-day life, I regularly check

in with my Elite Operator to ensure that I implement this state of mind and the standards associated with it, when required.

Examples of this could be getting up straight away when my alarm goes off at 04.15, and refusing to snooze; following my disciplined morning structure and not getting distracted; showing up when it's work time, rather than focusing on things that don't matter; showing up when it's Dad time, and not being on my phone; having the discipline between work and life balance, etc.

When I get a punch in the face from life – such as major issues at work, or the car breaking down, or the kids driving me mental (you know, the real-life scenarios) – I switch to the Elite Operator mindset and handle the situation. The way I put things into perspective is by remembering the mission and remembering what I'm trying to achieve long-term. This allows me to not fall into the self-pity bubble or the victim mentality when things are hard and it feels like an uphill battle. That mentality costs so many of us our time and energy in our journeys.

Over the years I have built up coping mechanisms to be able to handle the hardships that life delivers, and to be able to control the situation much more effectively by always coming back to my mission. It always offers perspective on the situation, and gives me clarity about what's happening in life right in front of me. My mission becomes my recalibration that centres me for what I'm trying to achieve. It really helps to put perspective on the external factors of life.

Falling back on your mission

The coping mechanisms I've developed over the years are a direct response to me being clear on my mission in life and connecting my Elite Operator state of mind to that mission. Over time, this process almost becomes an automatic response, after conditioning myself to handle those issues, problems, curve balls, and the adversities of life.

This isn't always a foolproof plan, but what plan or system ever is? We are only human, after all, and we live in a reality where there are many uncertainties within a chaotic world. We unfortunately don't live in a world of straightforward successes that take us from A to B without incident or distraction.

Just like I do, you will have bad days from time to time. Those days when nothing works out the way you planned, or those days when nothing flows the way you want it to. There will be times when you feel like you aren't good enough, which is a situation that could easily get the better of you. Or you might have just woken up and found that the world is against you from the off.

The idea of the 'remember the mission' ethos is to bring you back from those bad days, to realign you to your centre, your path, your purpose. It's to stop a bad day becoming a bad week, month, or even a bad year. Remembering the mission reminds you that one bad day does not define you. One bad day is just a micro element of your life and mission, and a few bad days won't dent that mission. So, it's okay to have those bad days; it takes the pressure off us.

'Remember the mission' becomes your path and process, implementing your mission day by day with clear direction, like an Elite Operator. Implementing this ethos is what will get you up the next morning ready to go again; it's what will ignite the fire, the emotional connection, the desire and drive to go again, hungry to see how far you can push yourself, with no dwelling thoughts of what happened yesterday. Yesterday is done, today and tomorrow is the mission. I call this 'the bouncebackability mindset'.

Sharpening the tools

When I personally have a bad day or am facing levels of adversity, I often go visual, imagining I'm on mission again either in training or serving in Afghanistan. I go to what I call the 'green zone'. It's a bit chad, but it works for me and for many of the guys I coach.

I visualise myself with my green beret on again, Royal Marine Commando flashes on show, and I'm instantly transformed into that confident identity I carried as a Royal Marine Commando. That feeling of confidence and being unbreakable is what brings me back to my best self whenever I feel vulnerable, low on confidence, or feel that I'm slipping into a victim mentality.

That's when I feel I 10X my approach to life, dealing with adversity, and problem solving. Being in that mental and emotional state raises my ability to be my best self, and sets off the fire inside me to come out on top.

I was switched on most in life when I was on a mission in the military, whether that was a training exercise or doing the real thing when patrolling in Afghanistan. When I say 'switched on', I mean that the levels of focus, awareness, forward-thinking, planning, and structure, were at their highest. I was at the top of my game and mentally sharp.

As you haven't all been in the military, naturally it will be hard to understand or visualise this. But I'll share with you the way I've taught my coaching members how to approach this.

I want you to think about a war film that you've watched or read about. Think about that one character in the film or book who really stood out – the way he operated, the way he handled himself, the way he thought, and the action he took.

Your confident identity

He was clearly the guy everyone would love to be. When faced with a tough decision, he'd quite often be the guy you'd ask yourself, *What would he do?* He was always in control, calm, and clear on what he was doing. He could make a decision and action it with full commitment. Sure, he was a fictional character, but so is your alter ego. Does the Elite Operator come to mind? It's not so much the image, but the character shown and the attitude to getting things done.

I realise this probably sounds like a *Call of Duty* game,

where you are creating your own avatar, but what I'm trying to do is create a vision or image with emotion, a state of mind, and attitude; a character that is going to help you achieve your mission. So, in some ways you are creating a character that's going to help you show up to that mission. And with that character will come principles and values that will carry you through the process.

For so long you've been guided by your chimp, ego, and impulse, making you mostly reactive rather than proactive. But there has to be a counter to the way you are thinking and acting. If you can embrace and adapt this alter ego that fills you with confidence and that makes you feel focused and unbreakable, then it's going to help you achieve your own mission when things get tough. And they *will* get tough.

Win the war, not all the battles

We obviously are not going to war, but your life can sometimes feel like that. Relationship dramas, work dilemmas, self-sabotage setbacks, all attack your mind and emotions in your everyday life. These are battles you must win, but you need to be in the right mindset to do so. Otherwise, you become an army without the weapons to fight back.

Imagine the rest of your life being a war, and the day-to-day activities of your life as the various battles in that conflict. Each battle won takes you a step closer to winning your war. And the mission is about winning the war. Not every battle can be won, but if you don't show up to fight back after losing a battle, then you have no chance of winning the war.

There are four pillars to win at, which I talk about in depth in my first book, *It's a State of Mind.* They are:

- Health
- Relationships
- Personal development
- Business

By creating your mission, you are forming your why; your purpose to show up. The mission will help you create the identity you long for, and to discover your potential, so the sky really is the limit. But if you slack on your mission, you'll lose your battles and slowly lose the war – and that is not the path you want. It results in unhappiness, stress, frustration, and bad habits.

Passion to the mission

The official meaning of passion is *'strong and barely controllable emotion'*. And the key word here is 'emotion'.

I've found that one of the biggest factors that men are missing in their lives is the lack of positive passion being shown. If you observed the actions of men – and I have done this with thousands of men coming through my world – you could argue that the only things men are passionate about are self-sabotage, being miserable, football, and sex. With the first two, I'm being sarcastic, but a lot of men do seem to just continuously sabotage themselves and are miserable.

I want you to imagine waking up in the morning and feeling passionate about attacking your day; I mean really ready to get into the day. Imagine getting to Sunday night and being fired up for the week, rather than dreading what's ahead.

Many people create missions for their lives, but they are weak missions that don't emotionally stimulate them. So when it comes to showing up when the chips are down, they have no emotional drive to get them over the line.

Motivation is not a permanent emotion; you can't always be motivated. Like happiness or sadness, it comes and goes in your life. And when it goes, you're left hanging, with no deeper passion to leverage your action on. So, finding meaning and emotion in your actions is much more powerful than motivation.

And connecting yourself to a passionate mission means you are 10 times more likely to show up!

That spark of emotion

I want you to remember how you felt when you met that one girl or guy you were crazy about. Think about when you first met them. It sent an electrical shock through your body. You were digging out on the dates, and when you kissed for the first time, it was chemistry.

That's passion; that's what it feels like. You completely

immerse yourself emotionally in something. You find new heights when you have emotion. New levels of action are found and barriers are broken with passion.

Now, take those feelings of excitement, passion, and desire, and create a mission that recreates those feelings – and remember the connection to the mission. Visualise that mission, the process, the feeling of success at the end. You can then start with the end in mind, and connect to that spark each day through your morning routine: journaling, general process, review, and reflection. This keeps you constantly aligned to the mission, and the passion to achieve it.

When you don't feel like showing up, when you've had a bad day, or feel overwhelmed, or are struggling for confidence, you have to remember the mission and what you are trying to achieve. Why you are not showing up now is because there is no passion to your mission. There might not even be a mission!

I've seen football supporters showing more passion for their team to win than they do about their own lives. If you are a football fan, or any type of fan, surely you should be showing the same levels of passion you have for your team, and transferring that passion to winning in your own life?

Constant reminders

It's really easy to forget what the mission is. You can write a whole bunch of outcomes that you want to achieve, lay out your plans and your path, and that will feel pretty awesome. You'll feel accomplished, like you are doing something with your life, as though you are making progress and gaining clarity about your development as a man. More control, more consistency, and more clarity.

A week later… you could easily forget all of those well laid-out plans.

I've seen it happen over and over again. Instead of the mission and plan having any meaning, it just becomes more lost promises and words, buried and lost in the chaos of life. It's a common pattern for many men, and one I've experienced myself. I truly believe it's because you forget why you are showing up.

I talked a few paragraphs back about constantly aligning yourself to a mission, being aware of what's at stake if you don't show up, and the consequences of not fulfilling your mission. You just can't afford to put yourself on the back burner.

Think about when you go shopping. You're convinced you'll remember everything you need, but there are so many distractions along the way that you forget. And if you arrive without a shopping list, you end up wandering round the supermarket full of products, while your mind is trying to visualise your kitchen cupboards, desperately trying to remember what you have and don't have.

But if you go to the shop with a list, and keep referring to it, you have a constant and clear reminder of what needs to be bought.

This scenario highlights the need not only for constant

reminders, but to be well prepared and realise that we can't keep everything in our heads. Without constant reminders, you will forget, slowly disconnect from your mission, and slip back into old ways.

It's easy to forget, through the daily chaos and distractions of life, and that's why I like to journal to help bring me back to my path. I also connect to it in the morning routine, transition procedure, and in my daily reviews and reflections. Just like the shopping list, it helps me to review and focus my time and energy on connecting with the mission, making it a permanent fixture in my life, in my mindset, making it a constant thought, and ensuring that I'm not drifting from the path I've chosen. And that's what I want for you.

The journal, routines, and planning become the shopping list for me to refer back to, rather than keeping everything in my head or letting it drift. I first introduced these concepts in my earlier book, *It's a State of Mind,* and it's vital to understand the importance of these rituals.

Let's face the issues

I want you to align your mindset and your mission to this process, so that you can embed it into your brain and it becomes automatic, like it's in your DNA.

Right now, you may be in the process of just roller-coastering through life, through the mornings, the day, the evening routine, your goals, and relationships. You start something but never finish it or remain consistent. Maybe you are always up and down with your routines and commitment to win this battle of change, due to habit, external factors, or just forgetting your mission. Maybe you haven't even started, or you haven't reached the next level that you are so desperately seeking.

Everyday realities happen, and quite often this causes a lot of the chaos we feel, because you become distracted and lose control. You start to slowly spiral into a rut, which often leads to those emotions of feeling sorry for yourself again. The victim mentality creeps back in, and you tend to bury your head in the sand, or run away from the issues, or drown the problems with booze, or shout at people you love. This might sound extreme, but I see these traits over and over again, and you've got to break the pattern if you are ever going to reach the Elite Operator standard you have set yourself.

If you continue on this path and keep running away from the issues, rather than facing them head on, life is going to eat you up and spit you out. It might not be happening right now, but you can't outrun what happens down the line. Your mental and emotional state will be consumed with unsolved problems, with living a false life, with running away from the issues that aren't going anywhere.

It's important to try not to focus on the negatives around you; to stop trying to solve everything outside of your control. Otherwise, all that happens is you burn up time and energy trying to control areas of your life that you have no control of, and that's exhausting.

Let's start dissecting positives, opportunities, and learning points from what's going on around you. I'm a great believer that you follow what you focus on. So, if you are focusing on the negative patterns of other people, others' habits, the government, the news, external factors, constant distractions, etc. – that's all you will focus on. That's where you'll direct your effort and energy, and you'll be left mentally and emotionally drained.

Instead, you have to focus on *you*, what *you* have control over, how *you* handle the world and go about your business, how optimistic *you* can be, and what opportunities are available.

The process

What I'm going to suggest isn't going to be easy, nor is it a quick fix. But to me, the key to your success is immersing yourself in a process, and following that process until the day you die.

When you are following a process, you are following a series of events that will eventually lead to an outcome you desire. And that brings direction, consistency, control, and clarity to your mission. You might be putting yourself in a situation that takes you out of your comfort zone, facing something that you may not have done for a while, causing you anxiety and fear, making you feel vulnerable and, more than likely, exposing you to failure. But that is a good thing!

As a result of failing more, you will be developing,

learning, and becoming more resilient and robust to deal with the struggles and battles of life. You'll be creating your Elite Operator personality. Through the process, you'll be finding out who you really are, what your character is like, and building clarity about what type of identity you're becoming.

In theory, you'll be starting the process of learning, growing, and being able to repeat that process. But we can only do that by putting ourselves on the line and failing more, in a bid to learn more and grow further.

When you don't have a process of your own that you're following, you tend to fall down amongst the chaos that life throws at you. You become swallowed up by toxic and negative people and environments, consumed by external distractions and destructive coping mechanisms, such as booze, drugs, or food. You fail to know who you really are and where your life is heading. You feel as though your life has no meaning to it. I've experienced this myself, and witnessed many other guys go through the same scenarios and mindset.

There are always going to be people who try to drag you back down. There will be days when you have a lack of desire and passion to show up. The hardships of life will probably never change, and you'll find yourself accepting those punches in the face from life without fighting back.

However, the one thing that *can* change is *you* and your attitude, mindset, and character when you face these situations. I'm guessing you're reading this book right now because you want to have better control and more consistency in being able to stay on top. So, why are you letting life punch you in the face and doing nothing about it? What's happening to stop you showing up?

If I came up to you in the street and started swinging, I'm sure you'd fight back to defend yourself, yeah? So why aren't you doing that with your life now, instead of hiding behind the bottle, or the masks you wear, or the excuses you make up?

You need a process, you need order, structure, and the long-term mission to remind you to show up every day, so that you are not being overpowered by the chaos all of the time. An Elite Operator without a mission is like a soldier without a gun.

So, it's time to create the mission and build your process.

The long-term mission

When I was 15, my teacher asked me where I saw myself in ten years' time. Until that point, I had never thought that far into my future. The furthest I had considered was a couple of years, with college on the horizon. Even now, 25 years later, I can still remember the thought process I went through when I was asked the question. In the end, I replied that I wanted to be a pilot because I wanted to travel the world. But the truth is, I had absolutely no idea. I was 15, and couldn't possibly imagine where I'd be at 25 years old.

I expect you'll experience the same feelings as I did when I ask you that same question. But I want you to spend the next few days visualising where you'd like to be ten years from now.

I use the word visualise and don't mention goals, because vision has more flexibility. It allows you to use your imagination, be creative, and be ambitious; it doesn't set the pressure of concrete goals that will undoubtedly change over a long period of time. So, just flirt with visions of where you'd like to be in each of the four pillars – health, relationships, personal development, and business. Then I'll give you a concrete task to follow at the end of the chapter.

A vision is a great way to emotionally connect with your mission. It allows you to picture the direction you want your life to go in, and you can see the stepping stones of how you can progress your life. It's not as fixed as a set goal because it allows flexibility in your thinking, but it nevertheless creates a powerful image of how you see your life progressing.

The goals are what we focus more on at the beginning of your ten years, when you've reverse-engineered the process. For example, to achieve a 10-year vision, you might set goals to reach a milestone in 12 months from now, then quarterly, weekly, and daily. These are all micro-steps to making the vision – i.e. your mission – a reality.

On those days when you are feeling lost and unguided, when you have the dark cloud in your mind or have just had a bad day and don't feel you want to show up, you can then come back to this mission you've created. Remember the mission; it almost becomes your blueprint to the bigger picture, which in time will help you put a lot of your day-to-day dramas into perspective.

It helps you to see the bigger issues going on in your life, and takes your pattern of thought to more long-term strategy rather than the quick fix. When you are working to a longer-term process, the small micro distractions don't seem so bad, and you are able to deflect more of what life throws at you and still remain focused on the bigger picture – your mission. It really brings perspective to the situation that's happening in your life at that moment. It's your clarity, it's your path, and you will form a stronger, clearer identity by following this vision and also the foundations you are building.

Don't have any self-limiting beliefs

One of the biggest barriers to people fulfilling their potential is the 'I'm not good enough' mentality. You limit your progress based on what you think you are capable of, on your confidence, past experience, childhood, or even comparing yourself to other people.

When I thought about writing my first book, *It's a State of Mind*, my own state of mind was filled with self-doubt because I did so poorly at school. My English teacher used to tell me I wouldn't amount to anything because my English was so poor, so I was allowing the self-doubt from my experience at school to stop me from writing a book. I genuinely believed I wasn't good enough to write it, and I still have elements of doubt about this one. I worry whether it will give people the value they deserve.

I think there is a connection between self-doubt and overthinking! But as you're now reading my book, I've obviously got over those feelings of self-doubt, and you must do the same if you are going to thrive like an Elite Operator in your own life.

When you set your missions, always be positive and don't doubt what you are capable of or what you can achieve. Currently, you are only operating at a fraction of what you are capable of, and you have much more to give. So, don't allow anything or anyone to change that thought.

Don't overthink

As humans, we have this tendency to overthink everything. We create statements like, 'If I write this, then that will happen', or 'but what if…' and 'I can't do that because…' And that's a huge contribution to why you are always anxious. You probably overthink being anxious, and create the problem in your mind!

When it comes to putting your mission together, just write freely about what your vision is because it's likely to change in some way, shape or form, over time. The purpose right now is to simply write down things you'd like to achieve, to find some clarity about what you want in life, and to show a little ambition without stressing about the what ifs.

Start getting your ideas down on paper, and start getting excited about the future again.

Where you want to be, not think you should be

Forget what others tell you, past experiences, possible outcomes, or social expectations of where you should or shouldn't be. You aren't trying to live the life that others think you should; you are living the life *you* want to live. It's inevitable that these factors will creep into your head and influence what you write down, but you need to ignore them. Don't worry about being judged or questioned about things you want to do. Fuck them! This is your life to live how you want! Elite Operators pay no attention to the noise outside of their own world.

If you work in a corporate company but want to own your business, write down that you want to run your own business or a side hustle, free of judgement or scrutiny, and with confidence.

If you want to travel for six months and it means taking the kids out of school, but you're worried what others think, fuck them and their thoughts. Write it down. This is about *you* being happier in your life, not theirs. Don't get to your death bed and regret not taking action.

Don't write down what you think you *should* be doing because society dictates that's the right thing to do. This is *your* life. In the last few hours of your life, you want to be able to look back at that life and say, 'Fuck, yeah, I lived. I did what I wanted, and lived life on my terms!'

Be ambitious, but realistic

If you have bad knees, it's unrealistic to write down that you want to run 26 miles; if you have back issues, why would you choose to say you're going to deadlift 200kg? You need to use a little common sense when setting your visions to create your mission.

A guy in my Mastermind once told me that he wanted to run ten miles in nine months. I told him to book a marathon for the date that he told me he wanted to have achieved his ten-mile run, and he did. As a result, he managed to run those ten miles just three weeks after our conversation. He did not have a clear understanding of what he was capable of, but as his coach, I did. I would never have suggested the marathon if I didn't think it was realistic. He has since completed the marathon and a 53-mile ultrarace, and has raised his own standards in the process.

You have no idea what you are capable of. So, find the balance of your limits, between what is too much and too little, what is ambitious and what is realistic. That balancing act comes from you being honest with yourself, dropping the ego, and learning about yourself as you evolve.

It can and will change

Wants and needs will always evolve as you do, and as your surroundings change. It's part of the evolution of being human, so expect your vision/mission to adjust at times – and it's okay that this happens. What is not okay is if you don't adapt when things do evolve.

As you learn and grow, you'll more than likely demand more from yourself. If you are following a mission and your environment changes but you fail to adapt, you're going to face conflict in the direction you're heading. And you'll become frustrated because of the lack of progress you make.

Having the ability to be able to adapt and overcome change in your mission is a key quality, and one you'll need to implement as you flow through your process.

CASE STUDY

Stuart had made plans for the year, based on his current position of being furloughed, and that included building a side hustle.

When he got the call to be told he was going to be made redundant, he didn't shift his plans. He didn't review his long-term vision now that there was a change of circumstances. However, this created a conflict of what he was trying to achieve, as he had a fixed mindset on the plans he had made... but in the old scenario. He didn't adapt the plan, and that plan now needed to change.

He now had to go all-in on his side hustle to build a future for himself, and that meant changing the mission. When he spoke to me, he was frustrated as he wasn't getting anything completed or meeting his expectations – and of course he wasn't! He no longer had a mission any more, because the game had changed.

This resulted in him becoming lost in his approach to life because he lacked direction and clarity.

You have to be prepared to adapt and evolve your mission. Things change; that's life. That's reality. And if you don't evolve, you'll be left behind.

Remember, no one's coming to save you; this is down to you.

MY MISSION

I promised I would share my mission, as it might give you a visual of what you are trying to achieve. I'll explain my three missions per pillar, and the reasoning for each.

It's worth noting that as I write this today, I'm two-and-a-half years into my 10-year mission. I set out this plan when I was 40 because I wanted to have focus and clarity about where I was heading as I pushed towards the big 50. I also visualised what I wanted life to be like after I turned 50, and reached the second half of my life.

Health

- Primary – Run a 100-mile race in my 50th year
- Secondary – Be mentally and emotionally conditioned
- Third – Remain in good shape, with good mobility

For me, maintaining my health is so important. Having the energy to keep up with the kids and work are important things I want to be able to do. Keeping my mind and spirit fired up and sharp is a vital asset as I evolve through life. That's why my 10-year vision is so simple. 'Fit for life' is my motto. I'm working on conditioning my mind and emotions via practices that put me first, like meditation, journaling, self-reflection and, of course, exercise. The point here for me is to get to the age of 50 and be ready to crush the following ten years. To have the energy levels to handle a seven and ten-year-old, as well as my two older children in their twenties. This was my thought process when creating my 10-year plan. And to add the cherry to the masterpiece, I want to test myself with a 100-miler as a 50-year-old!

Business

- Primary – Influence, in a positive way, one million men across the globe
- Secondary – Have three successful companies
- Third – Become a keynote speaker around the world

The key goal here for me is to be financially free by the time I'm 50. So, I wanted to focus on how that could present itself. By creating an empire of driven men, and bringing a few new businesses to the party, it allows me the opportunity to keep busy and constantly test myself in scaling these companies, and at the same time getting in front of people to share my message. It's important to understand that the business doesn't own me, and nor will I be sucked into it with the desire to be financially free. For me, building the businesses gives me a challenge, it pays the bills, it connects me with amazing people, and the 10-year mission gives me direction.

Relationship

- Primary – Plan and implement 6-12 months of travel with the family
- Secondary – To continue to be close to all of my children
- Third – To be happily married

The relationship mission is very short and simple. To remain as close to my older two children as possible as they grow up, to also have a great marriage, and enjoy a good relationship with my younger girls. We have a huge trip planned in 2025, where we plan to travel for around 6-12 months.

Personal Development

- Primary – Be scratch in golf (meaning my handicap is 0)
- Secondary – Have written a minimum of four books
- Third – Speak another language

The purpose here is to learn to commit in life. I chose these three missions, and in order to be successful in them I knew I'd need to commit myself to something I haven't always been brilliant at. To become scratch at golf takes dedication and hard work, as does writing four books and learning a language. Personal development is about improving on our weaknesses, and the mission that I've set helps me overcome that and improve myself.

Each one of the missions I chose had a reasoning behind it. Each one fired me up to show up each day; each one demands me to keep moving forward, making the most out of life. There's a connection, passion, and desire to push each of these missions every waking day.

I have this theory I'd like to share with you. I'm a very optimistic guy, and feel I can make it to 100 years old but be a fit and healthy 100-year-old, who is active, engaging, still sharing wisdom, and still enjoying my gin. In order to do that, I must ensure that I'm looking after the me of today to invest in the me of tomorrow.

When I say invest, I don't mean financially; I mean in terms of time and energy. The mission structures my time and energy to ensure I'm on a path, a direction, and that there's meaning to my daily action and milestones. I'm not lost like a zombie with no clarity or direction. The mission creates my North Star.

I hope that this can give you clarity to your own mission, help you understand the bigger picture of what you are trying to do, and give you a map with your new bearings and way of living.

SUMMARY

The mission is just another word for your why, or having a deep-rooted purpose to show up and make real changes rather than superficial, short-term alterations. I feel the word 'mission' is more powerful and relatable than your 'why'. In some respects, your 'why' can be forgotten in the shuffle of life, but when you connect with the mission and it's embedded into your brain, it is extremely powerful.

The word 'mission' actually means 'an important assignment to give to someone'. Well, that assignment is your own, and it's the key to unlocking your potential.

I feel that you can connect more with your journey and your process by thinking you have a mission to accomplish. It provides you with that mentality of knowing that there is meaning to your day, and understanding that it's taking you one step closer to the final outcome of achieving your potential.

A 'why' is scratching the surface of understanding the reasons you are doing something; the 'mission' is going in deep on those reasons, and creating the emotional connection. It's a constant reminder of why you need to show up. It's connecting you to your alter ego, the Elite Operator, who's going to help you make the difficult decisions when things get hard. And they will get hard.

The combination of the mission and the Elite Operator mindset, connecting and working together, can and will open up the pathway for you to have the clarity to be a more consistent, controlled version of yourself. And that's an empowering formula when it comes to change.

When I set my alarm for 04.15, I always have written down the words REMEMBER THE MISSION. So, when that alarm clock goes off and my chimp wants me to stay in bed, just seeing those words initiates the Elite Operator mode, meaning 'Get the fuck up and dominate the day!'

Without that clear mission and objective, it would be too easy to roll over and snooze for the next 30 minutes. But that just means you are losing your micro-battles, which more than likely means you're losing other battles as well. In order to win the war (life), you have to win these battles.

Your mission must give you passion and desire to pull you through when you feel down and out. It's about dragging you out of your self-pitying mood and your victim mentality, thinking the world is against you and that you've got it bad.

Your mission becomes your DNA of the new identity you'll create, following your process. That's the Elite

Operator in you, the man that shows up 1% a day, that overcomes the problems, avoids the toxic environments, is resilient in life, and fights back when punched in the face. Whenever anyone asks me for help, the first thing I ask is, 'What's the mission? What are you trying to achieve, and why?' If you can't answer those questions, that's your starting point to change.

TASK

It's now your turn to show the fuck up and create your mission. This isn't a ten-minute exercise. It took me a few weeks, reflecting on what I wanted in life, visualising how life might be when I was 50, creating a vision board of what it looked like. So, there is no timeline on this.

Some of you won't know where to begin. Start by finding a coffee shop with no distractions, have a pen and notepad, and start asking some questions of yourself. What do you want out of life? Where do you want to be? Remember all of the considerations I've mentioned in this chapter. The world is at your feet and there is no such phrase as 'I can't do that'. Here's a guide to help you put this together.

I want you to break your vision into the following four pillars:

- Health
- Relationships (personal for now)

- Personal Development
- Business

I want you to create three missions for each pillar. Your primary, secondary, and third target per mission. Check my examples and reasonings a few pages back to visualise how that looks.

To get to this point, I want you to brain dump everything you'd like to achieve in each of the pillars over the next ten years. It doesn't matter how long the list is. The whole point is simply to get you thinking, and when you start the process, your brain will start running wild. You've just got to unblock the mind.

Once you have your lists, it's time to start prioritising what the mission is going to be – what your time and energy will be focused on achieving for the long term. When you have your final mission, you are going to frame it and place it somewhere you can see it every morning. It will act as a reminder of the direction you are going, a reminder of why you are showing up.

Your final step is to reverse-engineer the 10-year vision to what needs to be done now, today. Here's how I teach my clients to do that. Remember, if you feel that ten years is too much, just make it five years to reduce the overwhelm.

Day	Weekly	Qtr	1yr	3yr	5yr	7yr	10yr

It's important to create checkpoints – or review points, if you like – to ensure that you are on target to reach your mission. The above chart allows you to then work backwards on your mission, and to create milestones to reach along the way. This can be done all the way back to your day-to-day activity that will keep you on the path to achieving the bigger picture.

This is where managing your quarterly, weekly, and daily plans is essential. They are all micro-plans achieving the bigger plan, the main mission in life.

You should now have a better understanding of how to go and create your mission. Maybe you only want to go as far as a three-year or five-year plan, but whatever you choose, just get it done. If you haven't started this process at least 24 hours after reading this chapter, the likelihood is that you won't do it at all. Be an action-taker for a change, and get it done. What's the alternative?

If you don't know what your mission is right now, it's not the end of the world. And if you don't know what you want to do, then now is the time to start trying some new things. If you don't like what you tried, then cross it off the list; if it's for you, then it's a win.

Get out there and grab life by the balls. Wallowing around, telling yourself you don't know what your mission is, is a complete waste of your time and energy. You find your mission by living it; it tends to find you. I can guarantee you, though, you won't find anything wallowing in your own shit.

6

How You Do Anything Is How You Do Everything

You want it all right now (problem)

You now have a clear understanding of what an Elite Operator is, and a better understanding of how to create your mission and why you must create it. I imagine that there is an element of overwhelm going on in your head, and you are most likely asking yourself questions like: Where do I start? What do I do? How do I do it?

Even though you have had some guidance, it can still feel overwhelming. You are also probably inclined to want to do this all at once, with the adrenalin running in your veins making you feel pumped to take action. You'll want to start improving your routines right now, the way you look right now, your relationships right now, the structure right now, developing your career right now. It's like an overwhelm of optimism, motivation, and passion, all crammed into one big firework.

Take a huge deep breath… and just stop. This is a

process with the long term in mind, and battle plans made in a frantic state tend to fail.

Your inner fire is alight, the adrenalin is pumping, and you want to create the new you – I get that. Whenever anyone reads a new book, watches an inspiring video, listens to a podcast or does anything similar, they are inclined to want to change immediately. But you want to make this a longer lasting change rather than the yo-yo alterations you're used to, like in this scenario:

Scenario

Steve booked a holiday with his family; it was three months away. Steve had been making bad choices for months, basically because he was under pressure at work, and he found little time for anything else.

Steve didn't want to take his top off on holiday due to the physical condition he was in. He felt embarrassed about the way he looked, and didn't feel comfortable. So he set about getting in shape for the holiday.

Three months later, he had managed to shift two stone. I remember seeing the before and after pictures, and was really impressed. Steve came back from holiday and didn't train again for two months. He then dabbled in the gym for a few weeks before becoming lost in life again.

This is a common theme, and it's the reason Steve

came to work with me, because he was so tired of the inconsistency. His health became a yo-yo, and he tended only to commit when there was a holiday to go on, or an event he wanted to look good for.

Take a breath

Okay, let's start by altering the approach with which we are going to change things. First off, let's address the quick fixes. Have you heard the expression 'buy cheap, buy twice'? When you buy something on the cheap, it'll probably break pretty quickly, as it's usually not great quality, therefore it doesn't last very long. And instead of investing a little more cash into something more sustainable, you end up with a broken product. The same applies for the quick fixes in your life.

The expiry date of that quick fix is not far away, which means it's almost pointless because you are going to be miserable again very soon, with the same issues creeping back into your life. In essence, it's just a temporary hit.

Here's another example very similar to our scenario: You have Uncle Brian's wedding coming up. It's in eight weeks and you are one of the ushers, so will be measured up for a suit, as you'll be front of house on the day, and you want to look good.

You join a six-week programme, and you smash it. You follow the workouts, you consume some crazy meal replacement over the six weeks, and let's say you manage to lose the 20lbs you need to fit into the suit. Great job! Well done on the milestone!

After the wedding, the reason you were showing up has gone, and you are left with no direction or mission to show up for.

Guess what happens? You go back to the way you were. Same habits, same excuses you used before you got yourself in shape for the wedding. You also practically starved yourself during that time, so now want to indulge in everything you missed out on. Within the space of three weeks, the weight has piled back on and you're back to square one.

Other than fitting into a suit for one short day, has the quick fix solution benefited you here? What's missing? Why aren't you sustaining what you achieved? Why have you now stopped training? Why can't you make it a lifestyle?

Following and implementing a quick fix misses out clear fundamentals and foundations to build on. When a skyscraper is built, the construction workers dig down before they build up. Without the foundations being put into the place, the skyscraper will topple over – very much like you and your quick fixes.

Creating the breakthroughs

Remember my example of the two men building their house at the start of the book? One built foundations, the other took the quick route and didn't. The second guy's house fell down! You can't expect to change any aspect of your life without the right fundamentals and foundations in place. This a game of patience and process, not shortcuts and hacks.

It's natural to want immediate change, but trust me, just setting up the fundamentals and foundations will make you feel as though you are progressing, and it will give you breakthroughs to show you really are moving forward. When I run the Zoom workshop at the end of the first week of my 28-Day Challenge, I always ask for the breakthroughs. And they are huge because they are moving you 1% in the right direction; 1% away from the old way of living; 1% closer to living the happier, more fulfilled life you want – if you show up.

With this comes more structure, less negative thinking, a clearer mindset, more resilience… I could go on. In the process, the men on the programme have lost weight as a by-product of what they are doing, but the focus isn't on the weight; it's on the mind, and emotional conditioning.

By building the foundations, they are progressing 1% a day in all four pillars of their lives.

The 1% rule comes into play in the foundation phase, and it's the daily minimum standard in your progression and development in your personal and professional life.

It's the minimum requirement of you to show up. And, if followed every day, forever, it will lead to a much happier and more fulfilling life for you.

Small wins to large wins

Here is an example of a series of small wins leading to a big win.

I started this book on 1st August. Every single day I had a minimum requirement to write 500 words a day, Monday-Friday. That was my 1% win a day. Over time, showing up 1% a day will lead to this book being published and read by thousands of men, helping them achieve new heights in their lives. And that's just by following the 1% rule a day and showing patience.

Here's the alternative – the quick fix mindset to getting it done. I could try to pre-launch the book in November, ready for January's official launch. That would only leave me three months.

I also have two other large projects that I need to show up for and work on. The result? The book would be rushed, the other projects fall behind, and I'd become overwhelmed, frustrated, and done with the whole process.

Remember, I'm playing the long game here. The Elite Operator tells me that I don't need to change the world overnight – just like you don't have to change every problem area of your life right now, overnight.

By showing up 1% a day, you're practising patience, thinking more long term to increase the consistency of your actions, controlling more of your time and energy, and gaining more clarity in the direction you are heading.

An example of this

Let's think about examples in your life where the 1% rule works.

I'll take the examples from my 28-Day Challenge. The aim at the end of the 28 days is not to be the final product. To suggest that's possible to achieve is unrealistic. However, we can establish some foundations that will make some big differences in that time frame.

How can you undo the years of bad habits, routines, and bad structure you've been following? How can you turn negative mentalities into positive ones?

It's important to understand that your journey doesn't have an end point; it's continuous till the day you die. To get out of the chaos you are in right now, you must work through each milestone by achieving 1% gains every day, forever.

The foundations I have spoken about are the actual 1% gains that turn the bad habits into positive ones, change the negative mindset into an optimistic mindset. The aim for the guys that come through this process is to establish solid foundations to grow and build on.

How we do that is by following a set structure that changes the patterns going on in your mind. The results come in the form of guys recognising consistency, control, and more clarity. They become able to raise their levels of self-awareness about what's happening around them, building resilience to the bullshit, toxic environments, and chaos, developing an enhanced focus to build the ultimate version of themselves.

And this can genuinely be achieved by following the 1% rule every day, forever.

The first week is like the shock of capture; it's the realisation that life has been shit for some time. Being asked to get up an hour earlier than normal and conduct a routine that benefits them, being asked to confront past decisions that led to the chaos, being held accountable for their actions. But this all constructs solid foundations and fundamentals to build your day on.

There can be a natural resistance to the process because these guys are not used to getting up, or being challenged, or in fact not being allowed to lie to themselves any more. It's hard and uncomfortable at the start because the truth is often hard to take, but it's a necessary process to move forward.

The morning routine may begin with the guys getting up and doing a few tasks that will benefit them – trying meditation, mobility, or going for a walk. Beating the snooze button – the 1% win. Completing early morning rituals – the 1% win. Learning what benefits you in the morning – the 1% win.

Is this now starting to make sense to you?

I don't expect the guys to wake up and be Elite Operators right away, or morning routine kings. It's a process, and during that process they – and you – will undoubtedly fail a lot. But it means that you'll also learn a great deal, which will result in you growing a lot. You'll gain experience and a better understanding of yourself, and you'll develop more resilience as you build your identity.

This is the by-product of you showing up 1% a day every day, forever. And the same is true for the rest of the factors on the course – the planning phase, the accountability, the mental and emotional attitude, the fitness levels, etc. They are all developed by you showing up 1% every day, forever.

At the end of the 28 days, the guys have become proficient in their morning routine, in their planning, in their structure and routines, in their awareness of health. It's a milestone in their process that they reach. But you can't get to that place after 28 days unless the 1% wins have been accumulated over that period of time. If you are not in the process, you're not learning and you are not growing; you are being left behind, and that creates frustration, anger, confusion, and vulnerability.

There is no quick fix to get to that stage at the end of the 28 days, no handy tips or useful advice to get you there. And that is true for your mission in life. There are no shortcuts to your success, and you can't quick fix yourself to happiness and fulfilment.

The next step for you is to find the next micro 1% win that will take you one step closer to achieving the bigger win – the mission.

Now look at your mission

I've given you the example from the 28-day process. Now it's your turn. How are you going to implement the 1% rule into your life?

First, think about your mission. If you were to break that down into hundreds of small wins, you would have a multitude of micro-checkpoints to reach. These are micro-missions that will create you and move you in the right direction to win the major mission. It's just about connecting each piece of the jigsaw together.

Your 1% gains and improvements are your progression. They are feelings of fulfilment; they are micro-milestones that you may sometimes undervalue. But these small wins are incredibly powerful. Sure, you won't look like you want to right away, you won't build the business you want right away, or have the relationships you want right away. But each micro-milestone is a move in the right direction – which is half the battle – and a step closer to your mission.

Here's some context

My mission keeps me interested and focused even on the days when I don't feel like showing up. I now have a plan that will offer consistency, control of time and energy, and clarity of a path... with the long term in mind.

What makes this mission successful is the small wins, the 1% margins each day. Like stepping stones, they move you closer and closer to achieving the outcome you desire.

1% wins would include:

- Completing a daily mobility set
- Listening to a podcast whilst running

- Joining the gym
- Completing a strength and conditioning set
- Completing a thorough warm up and cool down
- Beating the snooze button
- Scheduling your sessions into your timetable
- Beating a personal best
- Running new routines
- Meeting new people
- Taking part in new events
- Writing 500 words of a book
- Picking up a new client

I could go on and on, but these are all micro-steps to making this process a permanent part of your life. When I'm 47, we plan to travel for six months, maybe 12 months. The 1% wins over the coming years will be the planning, the budgeting, and building the business to fund our expedition. It's not just something we will decide to do and then head off the next day. When we go, it will be the milestone of years of hard work and detail, years of moving closer by 1% a day.

And it's the same with the business goals, writing the books, and being a speaker. Reaching 1% milestones like writing 500 words a day, building one system in a month to benefit a lifetime, investing in staff, building an email list – these are all small pieces of the jigsaw to complete the larger puzzle.

It's all about building up habits, routines, structure, and consistency. No more running for two weeks then losing focus or being distracted, saying 'fuck it, it's not working' and going back to doing nothing.

No more trying to achieve the world overnight, but understanding that more patience is required to achieve real change, that success is small progressions and micro-wins.

It alters your whole way of thinking and implementing changes. It's a carefully executed plan, with achievable micro-steps to keep you hungry and focused for the long term, without becoming overwhelmed or being distracted.

You are now equipped to think and implement like an Elite Operator. No more being overwhelmed, no more loss of direction, no more trying to change your world overnight. Just a 1% better attitude every day forever mentality.

TASK

Choose just one of your pillars.

- Health
- Relationships
- Personal Development
- Business

What's the mission for you in that particular pillar? Where do you want to be, and why? Base these questions on a timeline of a year from today. Visualise the bigger mission.

Once you have that answer, I want you to reverse-engineer the process. You'll need checkpoints along the way to ensure you are on track, and meeting the standards that you set for yourself. (See the example below.)

- Pillar:

Health

- 12 Month Vision:

Example… Lose 3 stone and keep it off

- Break down into 4 x 12-week checkpoints:

Qtr 1… Hire a PT, start training, and calorie counting
Qtr 2… Be able to follow a plan without a PT, have lost 2 stone
Qtr 3… Have signed up to 2 physical events, 3 stone lost
Qtr 4… Maintain success, embed the lifestyle.

- For each 12-week checkpoint, break it down into 12 x weekly checkpoints:

Week 1 – Hire a PT
2 – Begin tracking calories
3 – Start using protein
4 – Increase to a minimum 2 hours' exercise a week
Follow this same trend to week 12

This will really help you break down what the 1% wins are going to be each week. So, it's taken that full year's goal of losing 3 stone and turned it into a process which is broken down into 1% chunks.

A year can be seen as a long way off, and circumstances might change. Obviously, we can't plan for every eventuality, but we *can* focus on the things we have control of, like where you want to be, and the direction and milestones you want to achieve.

Think of the Elite Operator mindset to the mission. Sure, sometimes that mission will change – as we've discussed already – but it's better to be organised, working to a mission, and to be in control, than cuffing it from day to day, constantly firefighting.

The small wins are where the magic happens; that's where the 1% rule comes into play. In theory, if you gained one small win a day over 12 weeks, you'd have 84 small wins. I wonder how much better your life could be by achieving 84 small wins in a quarter. Or if you hit a 1% win a day every day for a year, that's 365 small wins. No doubt, your life would look a lot different.

Isn't this mentality or approach far more achievable than bombarding yourself with notions of what you are going to do and becoming overwhelmed by those thoughts and firefighting them? This way offers you a structured process of what needs to be done today, and the following day, and so on. And it brings you firmly in line with achieving what you said you would in a year's time.

7

Remember the Mission

It's all relevant

Procrastination is like a disease. It's a habit that prevents you from achieving your full potential. So, what are you going to do about it? More than likely, nothing for a few weeks at least. I have this saying 'how you do anything is how you do everything'. It means that if you're moaning about work, then you're more than likely moaning about other areas of your life. If you're slacking on exercise, you're more than likely slacking in your relationship. It's totally consuming. If you are putting things off in one area of your life, you're no doubt doing the same in other areas of your life.

For example, if you put things off at home – silly things like mowing the lawn, doing your laundry, putting up a shelf, tidying the garage – you are in the habit of procrastinating around the house. It's a pattern of action you've formed by the habit of continuously putting things off.

Now let's look at work. If you're in the habit of putting things off at home, you'll no doubt be carrying that over into your job. Putting off the email that needs to be sent, delaying working on the report that needs to be complete, sending out invoices, applying for a new position, etc. – you get the picture. If you are not taking action in your personal life, it usually carries over to your professional life. Why would you do something different just because you are in a different environment?

It's just the way your brain works and the habits you've got into, which in this case is your lack of action. But we need to start changing those patterns and habits to get you into the habit of taking action on what needs to be done. Once you do that, half of the problem is solved.

The experiment

For four weeks, I carried out an experiment. It was designed to help make me become much more effective than I was already being. I had noticed I was procrastinating on small jobs, which were building up to be huge jobs, and the consequence of not doing those jobs was becoming more troublesome. So, I wanted to get to the root of the issue that was frustrating me, and rectify it.

When I looked around the house, there were chores I had been leaving to another day. 'I'll do that tomorrow' or 'I'll do that at the weekend' was usually what I'd say. And it was simple things like leaving the laundry in my basket, not hanging my coat back on the hook, letting the recycling build up, not mowing the lawn, leaving letters unopened. You know, all the un-sexy jobs that we think we will get around to.

But these jobs became much bigger jobs, and in some circumstances the consequences became more severe by me not just getting them done – and all because I was in the habit of procrastinating. When I came to mow the lawn, I had let it grow so long that it took nearly an hour to complete, rather than the ten minutes it took when I tackled it weekly. This was a major ball ache, and a lot of time wasted.

Out of nowhere, I found I had three baskets of laundry to put away, and could never find my clothes because they were all still in the basket. It would take my missus throwing all three baskets on the bed before I finally got round to putting it all away. More consequences to procrastinating.

Not opening my post resulted in me missing important deadlines to return forms. Another headache!

While there weren't life-changing consequences in these cases, taking that approach to other issues could end up being a whole lot more painful, frustrating, and stressful.

More serious consequences

Let's say you miss one training session, the week then gets on top of you, and you fall into a chaotic state trying to keep up. As a result, you start to procrastinate about going to the gym or going for that run because you are tired and frustrated and it's the last thing you want to do. Through the frustrations of normal life, you've forgotten the mission, and you mutter those famous words: 'I'll start again Monday' or 'I'll do it at the weekend'. Aren't they the same phrases we were using to justify not doing the small things around the house? Same pattern of thought, more serious environment.

The consequences of procrastinating on your health are you piling on weight, feeling low about yourself, becoming insecure, suffering rising blood pressure, higher cholesterol... you know where I'm going with this. But that's how it starts.

I've witnessed the patterns around the action on the apparent 'starting Monday' that you promised yourself, and that implementation is very rarely followed through. What really ends up happening is that, before you know it, 12 to 36 months have passed, and you've totally lost your grip on your health. The early days of procrastination have snowballed until you're now struggling with health issues. And that's when the consequences of procrastination become a lot more serious and eye-opening.

Sound extreme? Sadly, no. This is how the majority of the men that walk through my front door have reached the state they are in. You put it off a few days, and before you know it, it's an issue.

Consequences in your professional life

How you do anything is how you do everything! It's not a one-dimensional journey, and you can't just be procrastinating at home then go to work and expect to be the king of getting shit done. And the consequences for this could be the slow decline of your business or your career.

I'm talking about simple tasks like not getting back to a client, thinking you'll contact them later, and forgetting. How many of you have received a text, opened it, and thought you'll message them back later, but never do, then realise a week later that you forgot and have to then apologise? It's easily done. Procrastinating on a phone call, or sending that email to a client or potential client, will cost you in the growth of your business – or your job, if you are an employee. Whatever industry, whatever the job, it's the same pattern of thought.

The consequences are much more severe than having to put away three baskets of laundry. Losing your business or your job because you've procrastinated on your roles and responsibilities will affect your performance over time and can be life-changing, having an impact on you mentally and emotionally. This really can and will affect the way you live your life.

How you do anything is how you do everything!

Take, for example, leaving a report that your boss needs until the last minute. You're risking your position because you've been putting it off, and you are risking letting them down. This puts you in a stressful position, and as a result, you're having to sacrifice family and personal time to catch up, and most likely having to neglect other areas of your life while you scramble to get the report in on time.

The consequences are unnecessary stress by putting yourself under pressure. You miss out on family time, causing even more conflict and stress, and that ripple effect spreads through the family. But you are the cause of your own chaos due to procrastination.

How you do anything is how you do everything!

Not changing the bald tyre on your car could see it blow out, potentially causing an accident. The consequences would be that you'd be late to work, or you or whoever was driving the car could be injured. You know it needs doing, so why would you risk the consequences by putting off what needs to be done?

How you do anything is how you do everything!

It's all relative. The same issues but in different scenarios and environments, and all come with different consequences. At the beginning, you don't really think about the consequences... until they have an impact on your life a little more severely.

This was my thinking when I decided to carry out my experiment. I wanted to change how I performed in my life, my patterns of thought, and my habits of implementation, learning, and conditioning myself to get shit done.

I had to level out everything, as there can't be imbalance. I can't be productive at home and not at work, so it all had to come under one umbrella. Otherwise, I couldn't achieve the big wins and outcomes that I desired. If I wasn't doing the micro-tasks that would build the patterns and habits and get me into a 'get shit done' mentality and routine, then how on earth would I get the big tasks done?

The thought process

My thought process throughout the experiment was that if a task needed doing and I could do it there and then, I'd do it. I needed to break that pattern of procrastination.

When there was any washing up, I did it right there and then; when my laundry was dry, I'd put it away, rather than letting it sit in the basket. I got into a habit and routine of sorting the lawn weekly, and emptying the bins every two days. There was some serious order in the house, and my missus didn't know what was happening. When I needed fuel, I'd get it when I next went past a petrol station, rather than leaving it till the last drops and risking a breakdown. In my personal life, I just got into the pattern of doing things right away, getting shit done.

I was building the habits, routines, and structure that

I wanted to transfer over to other areas of my life. It felt surprisingly good to be in control of my actions. It felt good not to keep thinking what I had to do, as 99% of things were already done. It was a mental relief.

This transitioned into my professional life. I started to keep my reminders on my phone. If something popped into my mind, I got it down right away so that I didn't forget, and I'd also put a date next to it of when it needed to be completed. Whenever I had micro-tasks, I planned to just get on and do them, and not wait till the next day or week and it became a problem because I'd forgotten or been distracted. Before I knew it, all of those 'I'll do it tomorrow' jobs were completed there and then, and it was such a relief to have everything all done and dusted.

By the time I had reached week three of my procrastination challenge, there was no more procrastinating, at all, ever. Over those three weeks, I had built up the habit of saying to myself, 'Just get it done.' And those words replaced 'I'll do it tomorrow'.

The pattern in my brain had shifted. The habits, routines, and structure had formed, and my behaviours and attitude to getting shit done had followed suit. Being so focused in my personal and professional environment elevated my desire to want to track calories and train harder. Excuses were now non-existent, and my positive energy shifted away from the once tortured and frustrated mindset that had been controlled by procrastination.

Over time, I changed the way I saw taking action, my attitude became much more productive, and I felt great because of it. I was feeling more fulfilled by having a sense of progression; I felt like I was moving forward. I was squeezing procrastination out of my life, and it was making a huge difference.

What's really changed here?

The 'how you do anything is how you do everything' approach helps you to recognise how you take action within your own mind, and gauges your levels of control in the environments you operate in. It helps you understand your attitude when getting things done, it helps you recognise patterns of taking action, and to understand the consequences of not taking action.

So often you are firefighting through your everyday life, on the hamster wheel of doom, chasing your own tail, and you don't even realise you're putting things off. You've become oblivious to it and the consequences it causes – some of which might not be felt until further down the line.

Like most negative habits, you tend to pretend they don't exist or become blinded to them because you feel that's just the way you do things and you've convinced yourself it's who you are. Had a bad day? Well, that usually triggers a need for a beer, junk food, drug misuse, or a cigarette. Feeling overwhelmed? That triggers procrastination. Finding an excuse to miss exercise? That triggers self-pity, and feeling sorry for yourself through the guilt of not taking action. And you might not even realise the triggers or patterns when faced with the various scenarios in your life because your head could be well and truly buried in the sand.

One of the factors I'm trying to improve in men is raising higher levels of self-awareness about the actions they take, or recognising the lack of action and the resulting consequences. You've probably become so focused only on what's directly in front of you that it's led you to becoming more reactive than proactive. This usually leads to a failure to see the bigger picture and to gain enough perspective about what you are or aren't doing – and I want you to realise this. I want you to win. I want you taking action like an Elite Operator.

The 'how you do anything is how you do everything' approach teaches you to show up that 1% a day to improve the process of achieving the mission. All I'm doing here is trying to raise your self-awareness of what you are not doing and helping you flip that to become more productive by changing your habits, patterns, and routines, to find a meaning to why you need to show the fuck up. If you procrastinate in a real battle, you would likely end up dead, or one of your brothers would. And although this isn't the military, if you keep procrastinating in your life, aren't you dying inside by not taking action? And aren't the consequences dangerous?

You have to understand that this is a long-term strategy. There are no quick fixes here, no hacks, no way you can suddenly change overnight and reach the mindset you need to process this. You can only experience this by showing up.

I'm trying to make this mindset a permanent fixture, and these are the early stages of you gaining control and taking action in your life. This is the groundwork that needs to be done. It's not sexy and it often doesn't bring instant success, but learning to shift your state of mind when it comes to taking action is the key to a long-term change.

Making it second nature

Let's look at the process of driving. When you first learn to drive, it's a roller coaster ride. You have to learn about the pedals, the buttons, steering – it's a minefield to take on board, and it seems at the start like you'll never get the hang of it. The whole process feels overwhelming, with so much uncertainty.

Think of this early phase of learning to drive as the initial stages of you wanting real change in your life. Everything seems overwhelming, and you have no idea how you'll manage learning to change your patterns, to be more planned and structured. It all feels unnatural. Again, it's like a minefield, it's hard, and it sometimes feels you'll never get it, as if every move is the wrong one.

Let's move to the time period of one year after you first get in the car for that first time. If all goes to plan, you are now driving around like it was never an issue. Driving has become automatic. You practise it nearly every day, and you don't even have to think about it; it's just part of your

DNA. What was just a dream or vision in those first weeks of learning, and seemed so unachievable at the start, has now become part of your everyday life.

And that's the point I want to make here.

I've worked very hard to get myself to the stage I'm at right now – by showing up every day. Just like driving, when you practise every day, it becomes the norm; when you show up every day, it becomes the norm. It doesn't mean life becomes sweet, because there are bad days – as there will be for you – but you will become better equipped to deal with those days, and have the ability and resilience not to make them into a bad week.

I still felt like the novice driver when I started working on myself, but we all have to go through that stage. Some quit because results aren't quick enough; some quit because they don't want it enough; some quit because they have no mission or desire to really want change.

But showing up every day means you have far more control of your mental and emotional conditioning. By learning to take action and not procrastinate on your actions, you are building this process to become more frequent. If you are an 'I'll do it tomorrow' type of person, how can you ever build the automation, how can you learn more about yourself, how can you get to where you want to be, how can you discover who you are and what you want? You can't!

One day, there will be no more tomorrows to use that excuse!

TASK

Now it's your turn. I want you to try the challenge I did.

I want you to do the things that need doing right away, if they can be done. Washing up, laundry, making your lunches, making the bed, clearing the car out, writing the report, sending the emails. Get on and do them.

Be such an action-taker that your missus won't know what's going on, and your peers or bosses will notice your distinct change in performance.

It's important to understand that I simply want you to focus on the tasks you usually put off. Instead of saying, 'I'll do that tomorrow,' replace that saying with 'Just get it done!'

Start by completing this for two weeks without stopping (you can do four weeks, if you like). If you break, even for one day, then you start the two weeks all over again. We are going to train your Elite Operator alter ego to eradicate procrastination. Your Elite Operator will now implement action at the highest level right away, all of the time.

Be aware, it's going to be difficult to break the pattern of putting things off, but if you want to change, remember the 1% better rule. Your minimum requirement will be following this task. When you are presented with something that needs to be done, you are going to do it. Instead of saying, 'I'll do that later,' you'll replace those words with 'Just get it done!'

How to manage this

You are going to keep a procrastination journal. In it, you'll keep a log of how you are performing at the task, noting anything you've procrastinated on, logging the progression, and the changes you are seeing.

Remember, results DO NOT come overnight. This is a long-term strategy, and this is just the beginning. I just want you to nail these two weeks, then build on that success. Our purpose is to build the momentum of *taking* action over *procrastinating* on action, to make it automated, just like driving the car, and to change the conversation going on in your head.

8
Identity Crisis

The prompt

When I first joined the Royal Marines, I was this vulnerable, inexperienced, young, 20-something guy. I had no direction and no idea about where I wanted to go in life. But who does at that age, right?

I used to run a fast-food restaurant, and was offered a position on a fast-track management scheme with the company when I came out of college. It was an excellent opportunity so early in my life, and the career prospects were huge, but I knew it wasn't what I wanted to do. There was always this burning desire in my mind that there was much more to life for me than running a fast-food restaurant.

As I shared earlier in the book, everything changed for me when I went to the cinema to watch *Black Hawk Down* – a war movie based on true events that happened in Somalia. I was inspired by both a Royal Marine advert I watched just before the film started, and by the camaraderie and brotherhood shown by the soldiers in the movie itself. And that ethos of 'protect the man to the left and right of you' stuck with me the whole way through my military career.

What I saw in both the advert and the film were the things I wanted in my life. There were identity traits that I liked, and which I felt had the potential to help me form my character and my values and principles – adventure, challenge, focus, risk. In that moment, I realised I wasn't being true to myself by living the life I was. It was almost as though I had a false identity and reality, and if I didn't do anything about it, I'd regret it for the rest of my life.

Within 18 months of watching that film, I was joining the Royal Marines as a recruit – and my whole life was about to change completely. The world as I knew it was about to be flipped 180 degrees. The process to reach that point had in some respects already changed me. All of the effort I was putting in with the tests, the five-day trial in Exmouth, the getting up early, had already shaped my state of mind.

I felt more alive in those 18 months preparing for a new life than I had in the entire 22 years I had been on this earth. Now I had focus, passion, and direction, and I knew this was 100% the right move for me, despite a lot of sacrifices that had been made to make it happen.

I genuinely believe that, now more than ever, having some form of direction in your early twenties is so important.

But there seems to be a huge gap in understanding and knowledge about teaching young men the importance of this. They need to be taught that the game of just chasing girls and drinking will end, and there will come a time when direction and a focus on their future will be crucial. Sadly, I think it's a major factor in many a man's downfall when they find themselves struggling mentally later in life, or even, tragically, with suicide.

Turning a boy into a man

Over 32 weeks, I battled through the intense and tortuous Royal Marine training, and my identity as that young 20-something lost soul was eventually squeezed out of me. On reflection today, I absolutely loved it, and it's one of my favourite chapters in my life. It created and developed the values, principles, and character that all follow me today, and I share a lot of them in my trainings.

The advert that I watched at the cinema, where the young lad went from that boy going through the water tunnel and getting stuck, to the Royal Marine on the boat on a mission, was so accurate in my case. And I was a totally different beast by the end of the 32 weeks. I walked around with confidence, pride, and an unbreakable spirit. I felt six inches taller, and had vision and focus for the future. I now had a mission in life.

New identity, new crowd

The lost young soul that had drifted through life like tumbleweed in the desert had finally found himself exactly where he was meant to be. Looking at a lot of the people I used to hang about with in my home town, not many of them ever really changed. Even today, a lot of them drink themselves into the ground, complain about life, hate their jobs, gamble their money away, and start fights in the pub. It's the same shit they've always done; the only thing that has changed is their age.

And I know that would have been me if I had stayed as the fast-food restaurant manager. Thankfully, the change in me took me in a completely different direction to many of the people I knew then. It's when we change identities that we start to realise that the things we had in common with that group of people have altered, and there is no longer common ground.

You will find that is most likely one of the by-products of creating a new identity. You will tend to be drawn to people who are of a similar mindset to you, and connect more with people you have more in common with. Don't fight that; it's part of the process.

Throughout the 32 weeks of training, my identity was always evolving as I developed in the military. The more responsibility that came my way, the more I had to step up, and the more my identity developed. By the end of training, I found that the people around me had the same personalities as me, and shared the same drive and ambitions. And that's what you must find. You will need to lose the people who drag you down, who don't want to see you succeed, or who get bitter and jealous of you moving forward.

What I gained from my service was a clear mission in life – purpose, drive, passion, desire to be the best version of myself, and to be around others on that same mission. I was content in life – actually, more than content. I was thriving in my new identity. I got to do amazing things with incredible people and visit fabulous new places.

That's why it hit me so hard when I left that part of my life.

Sergeant to civilian

I had no idea what I was heading for when I left the military. I was naïve enough to think I could just walk back into civilian life and pick up where I had left off. Okay, maybe not naïve, but certainly inexperienced. But I knew within a week that I had made a mistake in leaving the Royal Marines.

Imagine being on a cruise liner in stormy weather. You are on board a ship that's safe and will power through the waves, so there's an element of security. Now imagine being in a rowing boat, in the same conditions – vulnerable, uncertain, with the threat of toppling over at any second. That rowing boat experience was what I went through when I left the military. I went from a safe, certain structure to an uncertain one that could break at any point. And that can often be the same for anyone going through change, or evolving in life.

I listen as men tell me that they want to be like they used to be. They want to be that fit guy who ran a marathon, or how they used to be in great shape, or enjoyed a solid relationship. I can relate to this because I used to feel like that… until I realised that it didn't benefit me comparing myself to another time when the circumstances were undoubtedly different. Sure, I was fitter when I was 30, but I had fewer responsibilities, which allowed me more time to be fitter. It's important to focus on the today and the tomorrow, and not beat yourself up about how you used to be.

I look at my life now and never say I want to be as fit as I was in the Royal Marines or be like that guy any more. That kind of constant comparison was killing me inside. I needed to evolve by thinking forward, to reach my potential of tomorrow, not yesterday. I needed to stop thinking backwards and about what was. Unfortunately, it's a big mistake that I feel many people make. They put too much energy into dwelling on the past. You need to be in the moment and focus on your tomorrow, dude.

I want to work on the new and improved me that will be created through my process, and by learning who I am, what my character is like, what I'm made of, and what I want out of life. And that's the mentality I want you to have! Like the basic training in the military, I needed that process back in my life to help find *me* again when I stepped away and into the new civilian world. Creating your journey and following your process is what will help you evolve and clarify your identity.

I'll be honest, it took me three years to learn this. I failed to move on, to let go of a certain period of my life, and that left me stuck in that painful transition. I did my best to recreate that version of me from the military in a civilian world, but that mentality just ground me down. It was unachievable in my new environment, so I was fighting a losing battle and I had to learn to let it go.

Unless you recognise your situation, you may find yourself in the same boat, facing similar obstacles and frustrations. But you need to understand that you are a different man than your 20-year-old self, and you can't keep trying to be that guy any more. You have to accept your situation now, and welcome the new identity that matches with what you want out of life today, not in your past.

It's the same when you transition from another job, or leave a relationship, or move area. There's lots to embrace in the new situation. And sometimes, trying to recreate the old environment or not letting it go can be your downfall.

From certainty to uncertainty

The educational establishment I worked for offered me no identity because it offered no challenge. In truth, I hated it there. Many times I would stare at my computer monitor, feeling dead inside, wondering if this was to be my life for the next 30 years. I was almost back to having the same mentality as being the manager of the fast-food restaurant.

Don't get me wrong, there's nothing wrong with teaching – but it just wasn't for me. It wasn't the environment I was going to thrive in, or where I'd find my true purpose in life. I certainly wasn't going to achieve the new me in that environment.

Can you resonate with this? Do you know who you are, or where you are going in life? Or are you on a lost path?

Many guys face the same battle as I did – stuck in the transition of moving away from one chapter of your life, but never really establishing the next chapter. Think about men that go from living alone to having a wife and child. Think about fathers with children who have grown up and left home. Think about men who have lost partners through death or divorce. Think about professional footballers who spend a 20-year career turning up to training and following a ritual on game day, to suddenly having nothing to do. Think about military, public service veterans, who dedicate their life to a way of living, then leave and become lost.

These are all examples of how an identity crisis can occur, transitioning from one way of life to another and not adjusting, not finding purpose, direction, or clarity. Many will call this a rut, or being in the trenches. I was numb to this process and this mindset, as many of you will be. So, I buried my head in the sand, like many of you will be doing today.

Knowing who you truly are, what you really want, and what makes you happy, is the leverage to get you out of your identity crisis.

Knowing the answers to these questions is what will help you rise from the ashes of a chaotic life.

Knowing the answers to these questions will create the pieces of your jigsaw to form your mission.

Knowing the answers to these questions will raise your self-awareness to recognise the transition that is happening, and will be vital in helping you form a brand new way of thinking from what you know now.

Not letting go

I gripped hold of my military identity like it was the only thing I had because I was too afraid to let it go. It was all I knew, and I didn't want to come to terms with the fact that I had left the military. It was too painful; like losing someone you love. I buried my head in the sand and hid myself away from the truth, pretending it wasn't real. I was forcing an identity that didn't belong in my world any more.

But when you do that, you create conflict in your life, in your mind and emotions. Those very dark three years of my life were triggered by that exact process – not letting go of something that was over.

I see this so often in everyday life with men coming to the realisation that they are no longer the young, fit, 20-something that could run, or play football or rugby, without any issues; men dealing with the fact they are no longer married to the same woman they once fell in love with; men who used to have everything and then gambled it down the drain, and lost the lot.

Whatever your story is, ask yourself honestly: are you clinging to a past? Are you allowing feelings of guilt from your past chapters to prevent you from living and moving on to create a new chapter? Whether your issue is with relationships, addictions, work, or health, you are naturally going to evolve, but you must learn to drop the baggage, or you'll sink! Learning to let go of a past identity, a previous way of life, is the priority if you want to move forward.

If you genuinely want to change, you are going to be creating a new identity, a new state of mind, new values and principles that will in effect change your character for the better. But you can't do that by clinging to something that doesn't exist any more.

This isn't a two-week strategy of being hard on it for you to just slip back to where you started. This is forever, my man. It's long-term, sustainable change, a new way of thinking, and a fresh approach to your life.

I couldn't move forward until I accepted that I had left the Royal Marines and was no longer that person I used to be so proud of. I found it painstakingly difficult to do that, and even writing it today makes me reflect on how challenging it was to part with that chapter of my life.

You only live once, but if you do things right, that's all you need. If you are wasting days, weeks, months, or even years, dwelling and moping like I did, then you are wasting time on reaching your potential, and narrowing the time in which you have to be happy.

Learning and growing in your life is surely about reflecting on the mistakes you've made, and learning from them – not dwelling on them or allowing them to consume and dictate who you are today. Isn't it time you broke free from these shackles and realised your true potential? Isn't it time to reveal the true Elite Operator in yourself and to build this new identity that thrives in life, rather than just moping around and being punched in the face by events and accepting it?

The victim mentality, guilt, and self-pity will destroy you. Past mistakes shouldn't define you; they should create you. They should help provide the fire to drive your mission for today and tomorrow.

Consequences

I want to talk about consequences, based on my own experience of working on the front line with men. I observe, listen, and feel the pain when guys pour out their heart and soul to me. Many of these men lack true identity at the start – and you may be the same. That's not a criticism, just an observation. It doesn't make you below par or a bad person. It just means you're a little lost and we need to redirect you.

When you wake up every morning and ask yourself, 'What the fuck is this all about?' Or just see a cycle of life playing out in front of you: eat, sleep, work, repeat. Some call this the *Groundhog Day* or a groundhog life.

Imagine a hamster sprinting as hard as he can in his hamster wheel. The poor little guy is pounding it, and his heart is going to explode. He's given it his all, but he's got nowhere. He's put out all of that energy and effort, but got nowhere at all. This is known to us as the hamster wheel of doom: doing everything, but nothing.

Let's take a guy that comes into my world. It may be you one day, or maybe you're already in my world. You wake up, you go to work, you come home from work, you go to bed. At the weekends, most of you get two days off and then you go again. If you like, this is the 'shell of life'. Whether you are a business owner, shift worker, or your standard 9-5 employee, the 'shell of life' is in theory the hamster wheel of doom. And that could be your life for the next 30 years until you retire, then you'll play golf and go on holiday when you like, or maybe you'll end up looking after the grandkids as you wait around to die.

But what will have been sacrificed? What will you have missed out on? What opportunities have passed you by during those 30 years? Chances to have escalated the way you lived your life and achieved so much more? Your health? Relationships? Lost time and bonding with the children?

Within the 'shell of life' is the opportunity to make the most of life and create an identity that finds happiness, fulfilment, and gratitude, and that meets your needs. That won't happen every day, but it can for the majority of your days.

Can we nail life down to just three words? Happiness, fulfilment, and gratitude would be mine. Imagine having all three today, and for the majority of your life. What would having these three things do for you in your life right now? Would it make the process a little more exciting? Would you feel more content?

Imagine forming habits, routines, structures, and goals, and having the energy and drive to maintain them. Imagine having a mission in life that you could always come back to – one that gave you happiness, fulfilment, and gratitude.

You might have another three words that mean more to you. Love, progress, purpose, accomplishment, are some other examples.

Either way, by putting yourself through the process of finding *you*, evolving, growing, and developing your mission, an identity will emerge. You'll gain an understanding of what you want out of life, of what makes you happy, gaining clarity about a path you can follow and be passionate about.

Isn't that more exciting than waking up and asking, 'What the fuck is this all about?' When you have a mission in your life that you are passionate about, you have a process of finding out who you truly are, and what you are really capable of.

That's character building, that's powerful, that's leverage for change, and it's a desire to avoid the consequences of not showing up, becoming a lost soul, and falling into depression.

Be well aware that this process will involve failure,

without doubt. And you will have to dip your toe in as many different paths as possible. But by doing so, you will learn what you like and don't like, and that will bring you closer to what works for you and what doesn't.

New you

It took a major event to occur for me to snap out of the identity I was carrying around. At that time, I was unwilling to let go of the self-pity, self-destruction, misery, and feeling of being lost. It was an 'everyone else's fault but mine' identity. But I'm a believer that everything happens for a reason, and the events that led me to leaving the environment of the educational establishment and into entrepreneurship, were the game changers.

It was a process that forced my hand to adapt to a new way of thinking, a new direction, a new path that I had never thought possible. Being in a position of survival suddenly sparked action, passion, and desire.

I was faced with losing my house, and in theory living on the streets and not having a home for my kids. And that forced me to act and raise my game again. It prompted a rebirth of who I was, and my identity started to take a new shape.

The transition from one environment and way of life to the other, created a mission for me to follow. And my identity was once again focused. I felt very much like that young 20-year-old on day one, week one of Royal Marine training. I was pumped for life, excited, and hungry to learn… but very vulnerable and emotional at the same time.

Until then, I had never thought of running my own business. And I didn't have a clue at the start. I didn't even know what a P&L sheet was when my accountant asked (It's a Profit and Loss sheet, if you're interested!). All I knew was what I'd learned from spending hours a day watching every video on YouTube, listening to people who had been there. That, on top of eight hours a day working with clients, 24/7/365, meant I was just constantly learning on the go.

Through the process. I was making new friends, building a reputation for myself, and my confidence was high. I was learning about personal development, and developing habits, routines, and structure that were providing me with more consistency, control, and clarity in my life. It was all benefiting me, and there was a feeling of control and progression to my life again.

Very much like the military, entrepreneurship – I believe – saved my life… just at a different time. If I had never left that educational establishment, I would never have rediscovered my potential, as a dad, partner, and friend. And I feel I'd have just rotted away in a system that was not designed for me. I would still be in that office, doing the same thing year in, year out. And that wasn't for me. It wasn't the life I desired.

I wanted to live life on my terms. I want to be challenged, and I want to be out of my comfort zone. And I'm hoping

I can help you do the same, so that you aren't just existing in life any more, but are living your life and thriving. So many guys that come through my world are stuck in jobs they hate, but they're unwilling to seek alternatives, staying in non-productive routines that don't spark a fire in the belly any more.

Many settle for this dull and uninspiring life, believing it's the only way it's ever going to be. Many think it's too late to make a change, or to create a new identity for themselves, and accept they won't change. Many come up with excuses why they have to remain unhappy for the rest of their lives. But that's just bullshit, and most of you will know that deep down.

Those men I come across are stuck in that identity, some are so deep in a rut that they close down completely, have become like a walking zombie, and don't see the point in trying to change. I hear statements like 'It's unrealistic to leave my job' or 'I have to; I don't have a choice'.

Sometimes I think so many guys have forgotten that we are all in charge of our lives. *You* call the shots! Yes, of course it's tough, and I imagine there are elements of fear there about the thought of taking a new direction, but what about the fear of staying the same and being unhappy for the rest of your life? Remaining in a position of misery should not be an option. But that's where I want to help, by giving you that nudge to act!

The key for me was having that mission – a project and outcome, a path to fall back on. And it will be the same for you. I'm not suggesting you leave your job and risk your mortgage, but you could start that side hustle you've been thinking about. Look for other jobs that interest you, tidy up your CV, accept job interviews, sign up to that half marathon you've been going on about, introduce a better work/life balance to your life, take your wife on a city break once a quarter. Get the idea?

Do something that forces you into a process of action with a reward at the end of it. The process is the key to creating the identity that gives you happiness, fulfilment, and gratitude. Remember the 1% a win a day.

Still not sure? Well, what's the alternative? Keep sprinting on the hamster wheel of doom? Fuck that! Keep moaning about what's going on around you or not going on? Fuck that again!

Let's be honest, this isn't an easy process. Many of you will do nothing about the situation you are in, and many of you will ignore the lack of identity you face because it's too hard to change. But if you are not going to grasp life by the fucking balls now, then when will you?

When are you going to realise that it's time to step up to the plate – not just for everyone that needs you, but for yourself?

You are the main asset in your life, so you must step into your own Elite Operator mindset and create your own mission. And the identity you build as a by-product will evolve and shape you in the way you want it to. But it doesn't happen if you don't take that first step.

9

Your Perfection Mindset

It's killing you

I once knew a guy who always tried to make everything perfect. He had a business idea – a great one, which would have helped a lot of people in their lives. Behind the scenes, though, he was trying to create the perfect plan, to have the perfect preparation to execute the perfect idea. He spent two years creating all the content, programmes, the website, etc., taking his time because he wanted a perfect launch, and a perfect time to launch. He was constantly overthinking the process.

Eventually, though, he realised that he would never be happy with what he had set up. That once a plan had been created, after a few days of reflection, it would stall because of some micro issue that he viewed as being a huge problem – but that 99.9% of people wouldn't have even noticed.

That perfect mentality is crippling many a man's life. The perfect expectations of how things should be in one's mind can be a man's own torture. What his plan should have been was just to start the business, then over the years learn the process of refining the strategy as he went along. That learn, grow, repeat mentality.

There will never be a perfect time in your life for all of the things you want. And even if you do think there is, it never lasts. Think about the perfect moments when you go on holiday; the moment never lasts. I've often remembered a perfect family moment and wished I could stay in that moment forever. But it doesn't last, and the reality of life always creeps back in.

Let's look at a few other areas. The perfect fitness programme for you might last a week, then you get injured or the chaos of life gets in the way – and it's not perfect any more.

Think about the perfect running of a business, then Covid-19 comes along, and it's no longer perfect.

Perfect is a 'temporary to non-existent mindset' and will always evolve with time and the high expectations you set. The process, though, is forever. And what you learn in the process will take you much further than waiting around for a perfect moment to start your business, or your fitness programme, or asking out the girl you like, or even changing your job.

The guy I knew who wasted two years trying to perfect the business model was me. And that delay meant I failed to help thousands of guys to reshape their lives, inspire someone to save a marriage, or stop drinking, or even prevent a suicide. I have to live with that. Some may say I'm being harsh on myself, and maybe I am. My mission, though, has always been to help those that want to be helped, and for two years I missed the opportunity of helping those guys.

I had this perfect mentality and just overthought the whole process. I also struggled with fear of failure. I wouldn't allow myself to drop this mindset and just get the fuck on with it, and learn as I went along. What opportunities are you missing by having the perfect mentality?

I have driven my mentor mad with this, my partner mad with this, myself mad with it. When I started working with Phil and he came on board as my mentor, I just wouldn't listen because I wanted things done perfectly, or my way. I couldn't get my head around an imperfect way of thinking, and just fucking doing it. Just starting and then figuring things out was a tough process; it was like a block in my mind.

And it wasn't just business; it was affecting other parts of my life as well. Having the perfect morning routine, the perfect gym session or run, the perfect date night, and having the expectation that everything should go exactly to plan. I was setting my expectations too high, rather than being flexible and going with the flow of life. Being that rigid with my mindset, though, caused high levels of anxiety and stress when things didn't go to plan.

One thing led to another. And how I did anything became how I did everything.

Let's look at some examples of folks I've worked with and where these guys haven't taken any action because of their own perfect mentality:

- Finding the perfect time to stop drinking
- Waiting for the perfect time to have a date night
- Waiting for the perfect time to get fit

- Waiting for the perfect time to speak to a peer about an issue
- Waiting for the perfect time to change jobs
- Waiting for the perfect time to start a programme
- Waiting for the perfect time to start a business/side hustle

But there really is no such thing as the perfect time. You just use the perfect time mentality to justify why you aren't following through with action.

At times, it's a delay tactic in your brain, and you tell yourself you're not ready. But when *will* you be ready? When life is better? Or when there are no problems? This is real life we are talking about here, and there's no such thing as a 'perfect time'. There's always going to be something going on, some chaos or drama. So, when you can accept that, you can learn to overcome it.

This mindset becomes your identity, and I eventually realised that I was hiding behind the fear of failure. Instead of executing my plans and going all in, I would build up barriers of why I couldn't start, and that need for perfection was to protect me from failure. The perfect mentality became my excuse not to expose myself to failure.

Just start, then evolve

When I think of someone's Elite Operator mindset, I think of someone who's willing to start and have the ability to evolve as they go along. An adapt and evolve mentality is the ability to not worry about perfection, but to just take life as it comes and figure things out as they go, by implementing the 1% better a day rule. Eventually, the pieces fit together.

By taking this approach, you are not delaying the process of change, and you are less likely to beat yourself up when it doesn't go the way that you want it to. You understand that it's more about self-discovery than self-destruction, and you understand that your progress or success will not happen overnight.

EXAMPLE:

You want to lose two stone. Someone with a perfect mentality won't start until all of the jigsaw pieces are in place, and that means having a training plan in place, knowing what calories they need, hiring a trainer for accountability, ordering the right kit, buying the right clothing, getting the right days and times to train, etc. These are all great things to have in place, but realistically, by the time you've got all of this together, you've wasted 2-3 weeks fucking around, slipping in and out of procrastination, losing momentum and the will to carry out your mission.

The 'just start then evolve' mindset is about getting your trainers on TODAY and just getting on with it NOW, this minute. Not overthinking it, or waiting for all the pieces to be perfect. You are just wasting time and momentum. Start today with imperfect action, and as you start, you build momentum. Then introduce the pieces of the jigsaw to the process whilst still taking action. You'll constantly evolve in the process and journey, and the benefit is that you've actually started, rather than being one of those guys that says, 'I'll be starting a week on Monday. I'm just waiting for my new trainers to come through.' That kind of delaying approach and attitude prevents you from being consistent enough to see real change.

I've spoken almost non-stop in this book about the process. If you think everything is going to run smoothly and will be perfect, you may as well give up now and not even bother to show up.

The point is, you have to fall in love with this process; you have to become obsessed with it. You have to be willing to change the game, deal with the curveballs, and overcome adversity in order to win the mission. A perfect mentality will just crush you and your process, as I've explained.

When you have the long-term vision in mind, you do not become so bogged down with the bad days. You have permission to wake up and go again the next day, still following the process, learning as you go, and striving to achieve the happiness you've set yourself.

External factors – social media

The world we live in today is very highly influenced by what we see and hear on the internet – and, more specifically, your social media. There is a real tank of sharks out there, shitheads trying to influence their fake crap on you. The 'hey, look at me, I live a perfect life, I've got a great lifestyle, I never struggle' people. But I can tell you now, the majority of those people struggle; they just don't want you to see that.

Sadly, too many people fall for it, thinking that this life that's portrayed by social media's so-called celebrities, and people you know or follow, actually exists. But by comparing yourselves to these fuckwits, you end up feeling inadequate and shit about yourself. I know that because that's what it did to me and to other men I've worked with.

You may look at people you know personally, people in your social media world, people you know at work or at the kids' playground, and think they are living a great life, or that they 'have it all'. You make these assumptions because they come into the school playground, having parked up their flashy car, and they've got their smart suit on and their hot wife at their side.

So, you naturally make assumptions, overthink what they have or the way they are living their life, and immediately judge yourself against these assumptions you've made of other people. You just automatically compare your life to theirs, based on what you see or what they want you to see – not on what you know.

You have no context of their situation, though. No understanding of who these people you're judging yourself against really are behind closed doors. And we do the same on social media. We see people in great shape, putting their best pictures up, and we think, *Wow! They live a great life and are doing so well, why aren't I?*

Comparing social media lives

You'll end up having a conversation with yourself: 'Look at my life, it's full of stress and misery, so that's how I must be. How are things so perfect for them and not for me?' Enter a whole load of insecurity, self-doubt, and low self-worth.

But here's something you probably already know but haven't quite got into your head yet. All of these people DO NOT live perfect lives. Each one of them is going through something. And even if they aren't, you have to stop comparing yourself to these people because it's going to eat you alive and consume you in misery. Comparing yourself to others is the one single thing that will tear you apart inside and push you further away from being the real you.

Why? Because you will do your best to be like somebody you follow because you think they've got their shit together. You will naturally mimic others and their actions, thinking that's going to make you happier. But it won't! Maybe their strategies or systems will help you, but trying to live your life like somebody else is like having an imposter identity. All it will do is push you further from your own identity, and confuse the fuck out of who you actually are. And I speak from experience on this.

By the way, who gives a fuck what anyone else is doing or how they live their life? This life has to be about you, and you alone. I want you to leave a legacy that's all you.

EXAMPLE:

In my entrepreneurial journey, I've followed many people who've inspired me. I would watch hundreds of videos of them, but I'd end up sounding like them and not me. I'd use their language, their body language, and I'd try to imitate their product. Like an utter dick, I even got a website built so that it looked similar to someone I was following, thinking I was at the same level and would get the same results. I just lost a sense of who I was because I was so busy following all of these other people and trying to be them.

I reckon it confused me for about two years, constantly comparing myself to people who were running £100million businesses, and I felt like quitting because I wasn't reaching those heights. But I was setting unrealistic expectations of myself and targets, based on comparing myself to these other people.

I felt pretty shit about it all, yet I was still making

a difference to the people in my world. I just didn't see it. These guys I was following seemed perfect to me in everything they did. I thought they had it all and were living the dream. Now, though, I know better. I also know a lot of these guys were just full of it.

The way I moved on from this was to unfollow them all – all the people who were somehow influencing me, or taking me further away from my identity; some of them were guys I would even consider to be mates.

But I had to protect my identity and mental health. And the best way to do that is to lose negative people on social media, people who are full of shit. I even unfollowed people who were friends in business because I couldn't help comparing myself to them.

I look on that move as pure self-preservation. It has allowed me to just focus on me, where I am, and not constantly judge myself against others. It's a protective mechanism and one I'd fully recommend you do, clearing out the oxygen thieves and people who make you feel like shit.

How I tackled this

When I stopped following everyone, I was able to shine through with my own identity, and my own thoughts and ideas. I liked the fact that there was no longer any pressure. It helped me figure out who exactly I was and the direction

I was heading in. I needed that clarity, and I'm sure you could do with it, too.

I have also been really conscious of making sure that the people following *me* know that I am human, too, and that even though I preach about all the positive things I do, I still have bad days.

I believe I have a responsibility to do that. It's important to share the wins but also the losses in the day-to-day running of my life. That allows those watching me to realise that even the most disciplined of people can learn hard lessons, struggle mentally and emotionally, and not always be on their game. I want them to know that actually I'm far from perfect or have it all figured out.

Many people are surprised by the chinks in my armour, but just because I coach men doesn't mean I'm a ninja at life. They wonder: *How can this guy possibly not be on it all of the time? How can he possibly have bad days?* But that's how I used to think about the people I followed, and it made me feel shit about where I was.

I *do* have bad days, and I share them frequently. The reason I started my vlogs on my YouTube channel was to document behind the scenes of my life and to be honest and open. I wanted to share the process. And, if anything, this inspires more of the guys than the advice I dish out because they get to watch the journey play out for real. It provides them with the reassurance that it's okay to have a rough day – but it's not okay to stay in that place. You have to build the ability to bounce back. It's the adapt and evolve mentality put into practice, and this process is your journey.

So, while I believe you should take some wisdom here and there from other people you admire or those around you, you should translate that wisdom into being the best version of *you*, not a carbon copy of the person you are getting the wisdom from.

Acceptance of who you are

I find it interesting where our expectations come from. I imagine many come from our parents, partners, or other people we are judging ourselves against.

Expectations are the outcomes that we've set ourselves – sometimes unconsciously – to achieve. But I believe setting expectations is a skill that requires you to recognise your own limitations and to have an acceptance of your shortfalls and current conditioning in your life today.

You have to be willing to drop your ego and say, 'I'm not at that level yet to achieve that outcome.' Otherwise, you play on the need for perfection and fall into the trap of rushing the process to achieve the outcome quickly. You just end up setting the bar too high for the level you are currently at, and that's where the lack of consistency comes in.

Your current limitations in your conditioning will expose your deficits. And when you don't meet the unrealistic expectations you've set yourself, you become emotional and don't feel you're good enough. I call it the self-pity bubble, where you play the 'I'm not good enough' card.

EXAMPLE:

You set your expectations on forming a morning routine. In your head, you should be nailing this within 4-5 days; after all, how hard can it be? But the truth is that it's going to take anywhere between 4-6 weeks for someone that hasn't focused on themselves for a long time because you are not conditioned mentally, emotionally, or physically for it yet.

Think of the same scenario with running. If you haven't run for a long time and you expect to run a half-marathon in a month's time, you might end up disappointed.

When it comes to the morning routine, there's the adapting to getting up early, there's the getting into the habit of going to bed earlier, there's the nailing the activities in the morning, then testing and adjusting other variations of the routine. Then it gets to day five, and you don't feel like it's natural to you yet, the mornings are dark, or the pull of staying in bed for an extra hour is too strong. That's when most guys will either give up on the process, or stay in the state of mind that this new routine isn't really working and actually utter some bullshit like, 'I'm not a morning person.'

It's the same with fitness goals and career goals; you underestimate how tough this process is going to be. But the more experience you gain following your process, the better you are at setting expectations that meet your current conditioning. You begin to understand yourself and know your limitations. Those that win in the day-to-day battles are the guys that are more realistic and balanced about what they can achieve at that particular point in their lives.

It's all about matching your expectations with your level of conditioning, and not overwhelming yourself too soon. Instead of trying to get there as quickly as possible, I want you to think more long-term. And that's because I'm trying to get you there and have you never fall back, EVER!

These are the actions and mindset of your Elite Operator alter-ego. An Elite Operator is someone who can be honest with themselves, and recognise their own capabilities and limitations. They are able to move the goalposts if need be.

Patience is key.

Vision is vital.

Don't stray from the mission.

10

Motivation Is Wank

What is motivation?

There's a lot said and written about motivation. But motivation is similar to any other type of emotion we feel – like anger, sadness, jealousy. Those emotions come and go depending on the environment we are in or the circumstances around us.

If you see another man talking to your wife in a bar, you are bound to be jealous.

If someone cuts you up on the road, you get angry.

If someone dies, it makes you sad.

If you watch a motivational video, you feel motivated.

But what do all of these scenarios have in common? Those emotions don't last. You don't stay happy; you don't stay angry. The emotions tend to drift away as you roll through life, and come back when triggered.

So, if you are relying on motivation to get you through life, you are going to be massively let down. These emotions are like a hot water bottle. When it's hot, those emotions are high (motivation has kicked in); when it's cold, they are non-existent in terms of motivation, useless!

Blowing hot and cold

I remember filming myself for a Facebook live, running up and down a hill 15 times, and doing mountain walkers at the top of the hill. Every time I got to the top of the hill, I would get the guys fired up with some real motivational talk. What I was doing was filling up a lot of the guys' hot water bottles. I was leading from the front, and encouraging others to take some form of action that would hopefully give those watching the passion to take some action.

During the Live and post, the Live people would have been like the hot water bottle – piping hot, ready to take some action and strike whilst the iron was hot. And that was evident in their comments. Some said it inspired them to go for a run there and then; some said they would do something over the weekend.

Do you think they were still piping hot a week on from that video, or even a day after? The likely answer is NO. Why? Because just like the hot water bottle doesn't stay hot, we don't stay motivated. Hence the importance of the emotional connection to your mission!

Those guys that said they'd wake up the next day and crush it probably found some excuse and never showed up. I'd like to think some may have shown up, but did they continue to do so, or was it a one off? What do you think?

Come on, we are being honest here, would *you* still do it?

This is the cold-water bottle effect I was talking about, when the emotions have simmered down. Many of you will watch videos, read books, and listen to podcasts to get your daily dose of motivation and focus, to learn the secret of why others are getting and staying motivated. If those guys you listen to were honest, though, they'd admit that they aren't always motivated either. Maybe they do admit that. But certainly, not everyone on the other side of the video, book, or audio will be motivated.

We won't always be in the mood

If I'm honest at this point, preparing this part of the book, I'm not motivated to write. But I am driven to still get this book finished and out there to help you find your mission in life. It's part of my mission, so it's a part of me and my lifestyle. And that's why you need your deep-seated mission, so that you can still show up even when the hot water bottle is cold! You need something that sparks drive, passion, and the desire to show up.

When you say, 'I'm not motivated,' what you're really saying is you don't have a mission or vision for your life yet. You're a lost identity with no reason to show up. Based on my own experience and from working with thousands of men over the years, I believe there are three key ingredients that you may be missing right now, and I'll go over them in this chapter.

What is focus?

Focus is raising your levels of consciousness. Have you ever been driving when all of a sudden you wonder how you've ended up in the next town? You almost have no recollection of the journey, the things you saw, or even the songs playing on the radio. You wonder: *How did I not crash the car?* You were in automation mode, or another description I use is the zombie state.

If you ever want to see zombies, go to London, get on the underground around 7am, Monday to Friday, and look at all of the guys on the trains. So many people are in that automation mode – lost in thought in their own minds, as life passes them by. The unhappiness is hard to hide on some of their faces.

If we end up in this state so often, it's no wonder we struggle to focus. You wake up, go to work, come home, go to bed. Eat, sleep, work, repeat. You never focus on any other areas of life because you've slipped into this pattern – the conscious coma.

Any focus is usually on work, what needs to be done, deadlines, targets, and to-do lists. It preoccupies the majority of your focus, leaving no room for your health or family. Life is taken over by the emotions and exhaustion from work, and its ripple effects consume you and your life. When you say you struggle to focus, of course you do. You're not practising focus in another areas of life, so you have an imbalanced focus. And remember, how you do anything is usually how you do everything.

Put the focus reps in

It's the same as when you say you are unfit – of course you are, because you don't train. Or when you say your business isn't making money – of course it isn't, because you aren't focused on marketing or on growth.

In order to be more focused, we must first practise focus. We must put in the reps to make focus more automatic to see better results, just like reps performed with weights to build bigger muscles. Think of focus as a muscle – the more you train it, the stronger it becomes.

That also means being more conscious of what's going on in the other areas of your life in which you want to become more focused. You can't simply become focused overnight, in the same way as you can't simply become ripped after one workout. There has to be a constant process of being more conscious and aware of your focus level, and connecting more with it. You have to find the emotional trigger to become more focused.

Focusing can be seen as funnelling the chaos around you to make sense of the areas of life that need attention. Some may argue that focus is a habit we can get into simply by conditioning ourselves. In the same way as a baby increases their attention span as their brain develops, you must practise and build the conditioning that helps you focus for longer.

EXAMPLE:

You are a dad of three, living with your wife. You have a demanding job, and work around nine hours a day. The commute to work is tough, and so is your boss. Life probably sucks at times, and you tend to get drawn into the chaos of life, leaving very little time or focus on yourself. Now, if this guy came to me and said, 'I'm just getting by. I'm surviving. I'm drowning amongst the chaos of life,' I could completely understand that. I hear these comments daily from guys who drop me an email. Life is just eating them up.

My first port of call is to find some focus for this guy. He has no structure, no routine, and he does nothing for himself. For me, the focus is clear. I need to make this man more conscious about the things he's doing for himself, or in this case *not* doing for himself. So, in amongst the chaos, I'm going to get him to focus on a morning and evening routine to begin with.

The immediate focus will be on gaining more consistency in his actions, more control of his time and energy, and more clarity of the path on which he wants to head on. The Three Cs.

Getting out of the norm

What we will aim to do is break the automated unconscious patterns that he follows (his standard way of living) and break them up with conscious actions, such as the morning routine. That will allow this guy to connect more with himself and his mental and emotional state. In time, this will break up the zombie mindset, allowing him more focus on himself and his environments. Then, instead of waking up and slipping onto the hamster wheel of doom, or firefighting life right away, the focus becomes creating a pattern of events that will prepare him for the day.

Initially, we only want him to focus on the morning and evening routines, and not try to change the world overnight. By growing and only focusing on these two routines for a few weeks, the process becomes more manageable rather than overwhelming, and then he begins the process of conditioning his focus.

It can be overwhelming trying to change everything at once. It's almost impossible to focus on all of the working parts that will change you at the same time, which is why it's important to see this as a long-term journey. Remember the 1% better every day forever rule!

If you were a runner but you hadn't run in a long time, you wouldn't start running again by trying to tackle a marathon. You'd crash and burn, become injured, and lose confidence.

The 1% rule regarding focus in this case would mean that you eased back into the process, concentrating on just running a few miles a week, and slowly building up the process as the weeks passed.

This same focus applies when easing into better practices in your life, one step at a time. The more you manage over the long term, the better you will become, and the more you can focus on. Build your focus, do the reps, become conditioned, then move onto the next step of the ladder. Learn, grow, repeat.

3 key ingredients

For you to rise from the ashes and find a way to change your life, there are a few ingredients that are going to help, and you have to ensure you connect with these to find meaning in your actions. It's a bit like a maths equation. Connection + meaning = action = happiness.

As I've mentioned, you can't solely rely on motivation. If you did that, you'd be a yo-yo, only doing your thing as and when you felt motivated. And let's face it, that isn't enough. So how can you ensure there's consistent action even when you don't feel like showing up?

I'd like to introduce DPD – Desire, Passion, and Drive.

DESIRE – Official meaning: *A strong feeling of wanting to have something or wishing for something to happen.*

My man, if you are going to make this happen, you have to have desire to change. Why do you think you're on and off all of the time? You daydream of a better life while staring into the oblivion of a traffic jam, or when you are cramped into a train on the commute home, or when you go to bed and stare at the ceiling and think about all the things you hate about your life.

Fuck me, dude, do you want it or not? Where is your desire to change? When will that I 'SHOULD' change become an I 'MUST' change?

As I write this paragraph, it's 18.40 UK time. I'm 20 minutes away from coaching one thousand men on the 5-Day Fire It Up Challenge. I'm mentally fried, and I'm pushing the boundaries. I'd love to be home with my family, but it's game time on challenge week, and the only time I'll work past my cut-off periods.

I have a strong desire for this book to get out there and help change the life of thousands of men. Am I motivated? A little. Do I have the desire to achieve my mission of a second book and coach one thousand guys? Fuck, yes. Why? Because I remember the mission.

It's the emotional connection to the mission that many of you may be missing. That's the difference between the people who show up and those who find excuses to hide behind. It's the difference between being in the rut and allowing the chimp to decide what's going to happen. It's about being the Elite Operator version of yourself and making the decisions that need to be made.

TASK:

I want you to list five things you desire most in your life.

What do you really want to happen that's not currently happening?

1)
2)
3)
4)
5)

You now need to start connecting emotionally with these five desires, building a relationship with them, and finding meaning to them. The best way to connect with these desires emotionally is to ask yourself how they emotionally provoke you. Do they get you excited? Do they bring anxiety? Why MUST you achieve these desires? How will they affect your life and those around you? What will they bring to your life?

From there, you'll create a process, a path, and a direction, which you might be desperately lacking right now. There's nothing deeper than following something you really desire. When you have a real desire, you don't need motivation because you have connection.

Once you've listed your desires and connected to them, follow the second step, which is:

Understand your wants; understand your change. Remember that you are starting to form a relationship with the things you want to happen, rather than them being passing thoughts. So, when you know why you desire the things you do, you're more inclined to show up for them and meet them halfway.

EXAMPLE:

I have a huge desire to finish this book because I believe it'll awaken many men from their daydreams and help them create higher levels of self-awareness, saving lives, marriages, and relationships with children. And that's important to me.

That is the desire and the reason why this book needs to happen, and that's what makes this outcome a MUST do for me, not an I SHOULD do. It's the emotional connection I need when I don't feel like writing, or proofreading. It's the emotional connection to show up.

Your turn. Of those five on your list, write down WHY you desire them.

1)
2)
3)
4)
5)

PASSION – Official meaning (as I shared earlier in the book): *strong and barely controllable emotion.*

What I've seen and heard most during the journey of helping thousands of men, is the distinct lack of passion they have towards themselves. I want you to remember back to a time when you were passionate about something in your life. Here's an example to help you head in the right direction.

I'm passionate about helping you! I don't know you personally, but I know that if you are reading this, then you need something, or you're missing something, and you need to find it. I know when I get passionate because I can feel the fire burn in me when I get going on a video. If you watch carefully on one of my shows, you can almost see when the passion ramps up and kicks in. I go off on one and don't hold back.

I just snap into the cold, hard truth, and say it exactly how it is. It's an uncontrollable emotion that I can't contain. I'm passionate because, when I talk to you now or on video about a mindset or thought process, I think of that helpless man who left the Royal Marines in 2011 and ended up sitting on the edge of a bed, about to leave his kids fatherless as he planned to overdose. I don't want that for you. And that's where my fire comes from – not wanting you to go through what I did. I'm also passionate about BJJ (Brazilian Jiu Jitsu), about getting better at golf, about my kids getting ahead in life, and about my missus.

Past passions

Let's get back to the time when you were passionate about something in your life again. Was it the final of a football match, supporting your team? Was it a programme you followed to change the way you looked? Was it with your wife? Was it a new car you bought for yourself?

Connect with the feelings and emotions you

experienced at that time. Can you remember what passion feels like? Where's the passion for yourself gone? Was it ever there? Can you even answer that question?

Think about the millions of fans that love football. When we look at football fans in a crowd, we see raw passion. We see tears, happiness, elation. Grown men can create a state of passion about 11 people on a pitch that represent a logo on a coloured shirt.

Yet many can't muster the passion to change themselves! That says a lot about the outlook on priorities, or maybe the gap between what's really important and what we are willing to face. When you have passion, you are an unstoppable force when showing up. You'll do anything to achieve what needs to be done. So, use it to harness your actions; use it as fire to be focused; use it to battle the excuses, self-pity or victim mentality that prevent you from reaching your best.

DRIVE – Official meaning: *propel or carry along by force in a specified direction.*

Drive is the culmination of having desire and passion. Here are some examples to put drive into context.

You sign up for a half-marathon. You are driven to complete the race because you have the desire to achieve something you may not have done before or even thought possible. And the passion to show up and prove to yourself and others you can do it will shine through with that drive. You may be running for a charity that you're passionate about and don't want to let them down. There's your driver when it gets hard, and the going gets tough.

Being driven to make a difference in the world, by helping others, making an impact, saving lives and marriages, having the desire to make the difference, having learnt the hard way from years of experience and now using that experience as passion and being driven to make this happen no matter what – that has been a powerful combination for me.

Drive for me is the fire. It's the rocket fuel that most miss in the process of improving themselves. Desire and passion are the two ingredients together that ignite that fire, and the drive is the fuel to keep it going. It's the missing link that maintains that desire and passion to create your movement.

How it differs from motivation

Drive is different from motivation. Drive feels more long-term, which is summed up in the official meaning of the word – *to propel or carry along by a force in a specified direction*. It's touching on clarity, obsession to yourself; an uncontrollable force that can't be stopped, almost like finding your path.

You become propelled or carried along by a force. A force that is your mission. It becomes much more of a lifestyle change, as you create a real connection to the actions you're taking rather than always trying to rely on motivation, which you know doesn't last very long.

When you bring desire, passion, and drive to reaching

your mission, you have the ultimate recipe for success. The reasons to show up are clear, the desire to improve grows, the process becomes embedded in your daily life, and the mission becomes non-negotiable.

11

The Three Cs

You are not alone

On my 5-Day Fire It Up Challenge, one of the first things that you have to do is introduce yourself and explain why you are on the challenge. It's the first opportunity for the guys to be open and honest with themselves. From the thousands of men that have been through the course, the common ground is that they are all struggling with the same issues that you are most likely struggling with today.

And that means you are not alone. It's very liberating to realise that you are not the only one in a tough situation. A lot of this time you've probably been thinking it's just you who wakes up and feels lost in life, that it's just you who doesn't have clear direction or even understanding of who they are.

But I've been doing this long enough now to see this situation up close. Men are often silent about their struggles because their relationship with vulnerability, low self-worth, and low self-esteem is seen as a weakness or an inconvenience to others. The truth is often blocked by your own ego conflicting with your own perception.

Ask your mates

Quite often in a group of six male friends, 3-5 of them will be struggling, yet none will raise the issues they are struggling with. The thoughts of chaos in their mind, the lack of confidence to face life, the pain many carry from day to day, are all bottled up and dealt with through drinking, drugs, emotional eating, or violence.

I find the male ego really frustrating at times. It's this gigantic block that doesn't allow you to just reach out and ask for help or talk about what's really going on. Like sitting down with your partner or friends and saying, 'I'm lost' or 'I'm struggling mentally and emotionally' or simply 'I've lost direction'. It takes introducing themselves on the other end of a keyboard before many men actually admit there's an issue – and to people they don't even know.

There have been many times I've come home, buried my head in my partner's shoulder, and cried my eyes out because the day got the better of me. But part of my development has been dealing with those emotions and letting them out, rather than bottling them up and pretending I'm good. And I genuinely feel lighter for doing it. I don't give a fuck what people think about me crying; it's a human reaction. I know I'm not weak, and if you told me to man up, I'd happily choke you out.

Why do you care what people think in the first place? You are not weak because you open up to struggling; you are actually stronger, braver, and more courageous.

Opening up

I really want to be clear here. Opening up is a powerful breakthrough. Accepting your issues, pain, suffering, and vulnerabilities, and learning not to bury your head in the sand, can be leverage to grow. It will allow you to break free of the shackles of hiding the problems, and for you to be yourself. And you must do this to be able to move forward.

I know this from the experience of seeing guys opening up on my programmes and in my Mastermind coaching group. I literally see them changing as they get their heads around the reality of the situation, raising their levels of self-awareness. So, I just want to ensure that you know you are not alone, and it's not just you who's struggling. Try asking your mate next time you go out about how he is really doing.

Why don't you start by being honest with yourself? It only takes someone to start knocking down the dominoes for the ripple effect to begin.

The power of community

Having been in the military, I've understood the importance of community. Such quotes as 'you are only as strong as your weakest member' or 'we only move as one' used to really resonate with me.

When I set about starting the journey of helping men, I knew and understood the importance of creating a community – not just for people that invested in my coaching, but public communities that encouraged engagement and a point of view on topics I discussed.

I created a show called The Rise To Thrive Show, which runs three times a week (on Mondays, Wednesdays and Fridays at 05.30) on my Facebook page, which is called The Man Coach.

The idea was that I'd discuss a topic and give free advice or guidance, or simply raise an issue for the community to benefit from, then men could comment if they wanted to share their thoughts. For me, this show is a key element to what I do.

It raises the self-awareness factor for many of the men struggling to understand themselves, as I'm trying to help them make sense of situations, feelings, and emotions. I'm trying to break down the ego to allow men to be okay with failure, feeling vulnerable, and with being kind to themselves.

The show has grown, and a community has formed in which many will now open up about the topic I talk about. Just like the 5-Day Fire It Up Challenge, men are now starting to open up more through their comments, or even self-assessments of their own behaviour, which is brilliant to see.

Through this community, men are also starting to see

other men do the same, and that's where the domino effect begins. One comment encourages another to comment, and before you know it there's more than 20 guys sharing their experiences.

Programmes

I've already mentioned the power of the introduction during the 5-Day Fire It Up Challenge, but I just wanted to talk about the community during the running of the programmes.

Surrounding yourself with like-minded folk is probably the most important factor in creating growth in the individual. You become the product of the environment you are in, and those involved in that environment.

In the 5-Day Challenge, 28-Day Challenge, and my Mastermind, the community is all about growing together. They celebrate wins, pick each other up when they fall down, 'moving as one', looking after the man to the left and right of them.

I know for many of the guys that are part of the programmes I run (especially the Mastermind) that it's their safe place. They are surrounded by positive minds and voices, and can be inspired by another's ability to overcome adversity. It's about belonging to a movement that has a positive effect on your life. It's a place to share wins and lessons learnt; it's a place to feel safe and gain experience. There's a saying that you are the product of the top five people you surround yourself with, and that is certainly true of these communities.

When you are involved in a programme that's designed to push you, help you grow, 10X your performance in life, then you raise your game as a result. Being part of that community gets you over the line to the next level.

The other positive to being part of a community is the accountability factor. Many of you may not be backing yourself to do what you said you would, and there are two types of people – the doers and the talkers. How to transfer from one to the other is by having high levels of accountability.

You are not alone on this one, either. There are thousands of men out there who say they'll start on Monday, who'll convince themselves they'll start soon, but are really just full of shit, or maybe aren't in the right place, or are just not ready. Whatever the excuse might be, you can't hide from this, dude.

EXAMPLE:

Your kid comes home from school. They go straight up to their room because they want to get on their PlayStation. They leave their shoes in the middle of the floor, their bag in the middle of the hallway, and when they get in their room, they throw their uniform on the floor and get straight on with playing their game. What's the one thing that stops your kid from sitting on that game all night and ensuring they tidy up after themselves?

Accountability. You holding them accountable. So, let's see what that looks like.

You go into the room and ask, 'Can you please put your shoes away, pick up your bag, and hang your uniform up?' The usual response from a teenager would be, 'I'll do that in a minute.' But that's the same as you saying, 'Yes, I know I must start getting a grip of my life, and I'll do it in a minute.' So you are aware there's a problem.

But just like the kid who knows he has to pick up his stuff, you put your action off by using the excuse 'I'll do it in a minute'. And, as most parents know, that will not happen unless it's followed up.

The best course of action is to announce, 'Unless you get downstairs and pick your shoes up, pick up your bag, hang your uniform up, do your homework, and clear out your packed lunch, there is no PlayStation for the rest of the day.'

Now that's accountability, with consequences.

Where's *your* accountability?

Now think about your own situation. Who do you have chasing you up? Who are you accountable to? How will you stop doing the things that are self-sabotaging you?

The answer for many will be that you have no one or

no system in place for this. This is where mentors are so important in terms of giving you a firm boot up your arse to ignite action when you get lazy, to guide you, direct you, help create the mission, and remind you that you need to show up.

Why do so many fall off the wagon when it gets hard? Why don't many guys ever start? It's usually because there's no one there to help and support them from the start. So, those individuals struggle, and they follow the hamster wheel of doom, engaging in the same firefighting every single day, consumed by the same BS they encounter every day.

There are thousands – in fact, probably millions of men – in the same position, following these same patterns. And it's important for you to understand that this is a common thing; it's not isolated to the way you feel.

Don't be too hard on yourself

I hope after everything we've just discussed that you can begin to be a little kinder to yourself. Beating yourself up over where you think you should or shouldn't be is just destructive. You are where you are in life, and no amount of self-criticism or beating yourself into the ground will change that.

But you are not an individual case; you are not the only person in this state right now. And while that doesn't give you permission to stay in that state, or to keep ignoring yourself, it should ease the communication with yourself and the attitude you have towards yourself.

The communication that you have in your own mind can often be quite toxic and ruthless. You can be your own worst enemy some days, and punish yourself for the smallest reason. You know what I mean: The *'I'm a failure'* or *'I'm not good enough'* communication. The *'Is there something wrong with me?'* thought. But thinking you are a special case and that no one else is struggling except you is only adding to the poor self-esteem and low self-belief you've been experiencing.

This isn't an isolated case

You feel slightly comforted when you know there are others in the same boat as you. Not because you want others to be in that position, but because it reassures you that there isn't anything wrong with you, that the emotions and struggles of life are part of many other people's daily lives as well.

Self-love and care starts with not being hard on yourself, but learning to accept your flaws. And not allowing them to define you is a key foundation for your own growth. When you take away the victim mentality, the 'woe is me', self-pity bubble you have become consumed in, you start to ask different questions of yourself. Questions like, 'Okay, I'm not my best self, so what's the first step out of this?'

Rather than the 'why is it always me?' mentality, you have to raise your self-awareness, be fired up, and understand yourself in a way you haven't before, embracing the emotions, the struggles, opening up to them, and dropping the ego.

The automatic response

Have you ever noticed that when things don't go your way, you follow the same pattern of falling into the mindset of depression, feeling anxious, and adopting a victim mentality? It's like a habit. You become depressed out of habit; you have feelings of self-pity out of habit from a reaction of not putting yourself first.

You've created that pattern, that funnel of emotions triggered off the back of being hard on yourself. I remember always falling into that same state as a reaction when things weren't going well for me. But you have the ability to control that now.

Next time you feel sorry for yourself, I want you to recognise what's happening, awaken the Elite Operator mindset to fight off the temptation to slide into the usual mindset, and fight back. Building that awareness is half the battle.

The chimp, the ego in you, wants you to sink into the rut, but the Elite Operator wants you to control the situation. Count to ten, take a deep breath, and ask where those feelings are about to take you, then fight your regular pattern of slipping into negative emotions, thoughts, and actions… with a counteraction.

Ask yourself firmly – out loud, if you want: Am I being hard on myself? Do I need to go down this route? How can I get out of it, and put things into perspective?

Just by talking about this, you will already have raised your self-awareness to break the patterns that you've been falling into over and over again.

This phase of development can take a long time. Fighting ingrained negative habits and patterns is really tough – even mentally torturous at times. However, nothing changes overnight or with a snap of the fingers; this is about long-term change. Working on yourself will require a committed, positive, and optimistic mind, not a self-pitying, victim mentality.

12

Do You Honestly Think You Are the Only One?

We all make mistakes

Listen, at some point we've all made mistakes; it's part of the process of life. Those mistakes might have cost you relationships, your business, or career, and some will have been more costly than others. But let me ask you this: What can you do about the mistakes you've made?

Well, unless you've access to a time machine, 'fuck all' is the answer.

You can't physically undo what's happened. But you can make amends. You can try to rebuild the ruins of the mistakes you've made, depending how much of an impact those errors have had. While you can't undo the mistakes, you can allow yourself to move on and use the experience to help you grow.

One of the first things to do is to stop burying your head in the sand and thinking that the pain of your mistake will just go away, or that you can pretend it hasn't happened.

But you don't have to stay in a state of regret, depression, or remorse, punishing yourself for being a human being and making a bad decision.

The real kick in the teeth would be if you spent the next three, five, or ten years in that state, wasting your life in emotional prison, and never allowing yourself to move on.

You are allowed to be happy; you are allowed to move on.

It'll happen again

And guess what, you'll probably make another bad decision in your life. You'll more than likely make a mistake again, because we are driven by emotions and misplaced priorities. As humans, we act first and think second.

I always feel that a mistake or a poor decision is only bad if you make it twice. The first time is a learning experience, the second time is stupidity, and you haven't learned your lesson. But again, we are only human.

I've lost count of the number of bad decisions I've made over the years. In 2011, when I left the Royal Marines, I spent the next three years thinking I had made a huge mistake leaving the military. In my mind, it was the only certain thing in my life.

Today, I look back and realise that it was never a mistake; it was just my life evolving and me resisting the change. It was my state of mind that saw it as a mistake at the time because I went through three years of misery. Yet I'd never be who I am today without having gone through that phase of my life, experiencing the hardships, battles, mistakes, and poor decisions. They leave battle scars, which give us valuable experience on our journey.

Mistakes make you

Without making mistakes along the way, I'd never have the experience that I do today. I'm now able to change the lives of many men due to the mistakes that I've made along the way. I'm able to use that experience to help mentor and guide others in their paths. So, in that respect, I've channelled my mistakes into something good.

Unfortunately, that isn't the case for everyone. I see so many men dwelling on their mistakes and not learning or growing from them. Instead, they stay in that bubble and become chained to the consequences of what's happened, and don't allow themselves to get over it and get on with life.

I know that personally, having made life-changing mistakes that cost me my marriage, through my own selfish actions and mentality. And that affected the opportunity to be with my children every day, which was torture for me in the early days of separation.

But as time goes on, you see those mistakes differently, and you make the most of what's happened by moving in the right direction. You find the positives amongst the negatives – but you won't if you dwell on them and feel sorry for yourself.

Carrying the extra weight

When I was in the military, we took part in mountain training during the winter, which was a great experience. We'd always have our bergens rammed with all the safety kit and our personal stuff, which added to the weight and made them punishingly heavy.

One thing we always used to do was to unpack one of the lads' kit, add a 10kg weight to the bottom of his bag, and then repack it. As we were doing our hike, we'd laugh as we watched the newest guy sweat his tits off, carrying the extra weight. It was just light-hearted military banter – something that never got boring.

And, having been on the receiving end of that practical joke a few times, carrying the extra weight over miles of savage mountain terrain, it can really bog you down and exhaust you.

This is how I see men when they are carrying the weight of their mistakes. It restricts momentum, slows you down, and drains you of your energy. The constant slog of life, with the added weight of bad decisions, is totally mind-fucking.

I'm often asked, 'How do I get over a mistake?' and I usually reply by asking three questions:

- Can you change the mistake?

- What actions have you taken to reflect on what's happened?
- What have you done to move on from the mistake you've made?

Quite often, you know the answers to these questions, but facing up to the truth and even acknowledging what's happened is most likely your biggest block. Face up to the mistakes, make sense of them, then leave them behind.

The only way you are going to break free from the shackles and shed the extra weight following you around and weighing you down is by unpacking that heavy bag and dealing with the deep-rooted problem.

Regrets are the heaviest emotion to carry with us, but you can't do anything except learn from them. So, stop letting mistakes dominate the rest of your life, dude. Lighten the load and learn to look at life in a new direction, without baggage.

Looking in the right direction

You have two directional paths – future and past. When you look at the 'past' path, I want you to visualise yourself standing on a huge mountain top. From there, you can see the whole of your past. The mistakes, the regrets, and the bad decisions… But you can also see the good things that happened, when you used to be fit and happy. And those are the moments you want to hold onto.

Now, if you wanted to, you could keep looking down that path – as many men do. They stay there, facing that path, walking back down memory lane, revisiting all of the images, emotions of regret they faced, occasionally reliving some of the good times. So many of those guys live in the past.

Or…

You could turn around and face the other direction – one that offers you a blank canvas with endless opportunities.

I often watch my young daughter grab a piece of paper and start drawing, creating her picture, her masterpiece. And when she's finished, she puts it aside and grabs a fresh sheet of paper and just starts again.

That's how I see this new path, the future path. It offers an endless supply of opportunities for you to grow and live by. A place where you can create small masterpieces that make up your identity, your journey, and your process. And when one chapter is accomplished, you then grab the next blank canvas and start again with your new-found knowledge, experience, and resilience.

That path is a fresh adventure. The blank canvas means nothing has been written yet, which means your future is not yet decided. But it offers you a future – one in which you are in control of your decisions and your progress.

Let's fast forward 30 years from now. You've been staring down that 'past path' for 30 years, constantly facing the guilt and regret that's built up on the mountain top, and it's affected every decision and action you've taken during that time.

Now when you turn around, the blank canvas of the other (future) path is much smaller because you've wasted so much time looking down the wrong path. You've missed a lifetime of opportunity to create a new future. It's not too late, but there's less opportunity to create the masterpiece that you really want.

Right now, today, ask yourself: Are you looking at the 'past' path? Or are you looking to the future – your blank canvas, where you are about to create your masterpiece, your new life and version of yourself?

What's your next move?

Use regret as your fire

I have many regrets – big and small – but the only way that I've ever been able to move away from them or get over them is by using them as my fire.

The way I handled my first marriage was awful. I was selfish and a coward, and I let down my wife and my kids with my attitude and approach to life.

I was struggling with the trauma of adjusting to life out of the military, and I wasn't thinking clearly enough. But that's not an excuse, and I should have handled the situation much better.

In the years that followed, I spent many hours working on myself – to make me a much better man, to be more understanding, to think of others more, to put others' needs before mine when required.

The last eight years of personal development have come off the back of understanding what I used to be like, and knowing that I wanted to be a better man because of it.

The fire comes from those regrets. The connection to the mission comes from reliving those gut-wrenching, hurtful moments, and ensuring that I never put anyone through that again. And it's what drives me to be 1% better every day for my kids, partner, friends, and clients.

I do carry regret, but I've just changed the relationship and how I see regret. I can't change what's been done, but I can make sure it doesn't happen again. You'll have noticed that I always talk about connection to the mission, so what better leverage than to connect to those emotions that hurt you the most and using those emotions as fire to show up?

Life is an ongoing learning experience, from when your mother gives birth to you until you take your last breath. If you can't learn and grow from failure, regret, and past experiences to improve yourself, then you are not really living. You are just rotting inside, unable to let go and move on to grow.

That's why I want you to remember the mission. I want you to use the fire of your past to create your masterpiece – your life!

It's a learning phase

As mentioned in my introduction, in 2013 I started my first business, called Bodyshock Fitness. It was a fitness bootcamp, helping folks in my town get fit and stay fit. In the first year, I was like a baby deer in the wild – open to being mauled by a lion, vulnerable as fuck, and without a clue about what I was doing.

My learning curve was as steep as a skyscraper. But with a learning curve that steep, there are bound to be mistakes and failures. What I didn't understand in these early stages, though, was that failure and making mistakes is okay. But I very quickly learned that a failure was actually a win.

In my opinion, people don't fail enough. That sound crazy? Why on earth would someone want to fail more? But in that first year I would have never grown if I hadn't kept failing. I would have learnt nothing about running a business, and simply stayed static. I more than likely would have stayed in my comfort zone, and not achieved the success I have.

Remember what I said about using the regret, mistakes, and failure as your fire? Well, that's what I did. I was also driven by my local competitor ridiculing me on social media in the early days. And despite my mental and emotional state being awful, I still managed to show up – because of the fire of everything that was happening around me.

I was learning that my work ethic came off the back of proving people wrong and the mistakes I made along the way. I multiplied my efforts to rectify those mistakes and prove to myself, and others, that I could see this through.

I was willing to outwork my competitors by using the fire that was there every morning when I woke up. Every day was a learning day, raising my levels of self-awareness, realising what wasn't working and changing the pattern to make it work, refusing to stay on a losing path.

What I see in so many men is the lack of learning. We've all heard people say, 'I'm on it Monday', 'I'm not drinking any more', 'I'm eating well now', or 'I'm improving my work-life balance'... only to fall at the same hurdle week in, week out. Quite often, when someone follows that same path over and over again with no success, it's a key indicator that something has to change to make this work more efficiently.

But making that decision, or change, doesn't happen for many. I personally feel that's due to a combination of ego, unwillingness to invest in oneself to learn, no idea how to start, and a lack of self-confidence.

This book is aimed at helping you to really start to know and understand yourself better. Having the self-awareness to understand that your approach isn't working, and learning from what you've been trying to do, is a powerful process.

It means you are willing to do anything to make this work and not stay on the same tired path that isn't working.

TASK:

I want you to write down this mantra:

LEARN – GROW – REPEAT

This is what you'll live by. When something happens in your life, you'll no longer live by the fear of failure, but be brave enough to make a decision that will benefit you, and not fear the outcome.

And if it doesn't work out, then you'll learn, grow, and go again – without overthinking, without fear of trying again, without judgement. You'll understand that it's all part of the mission, part of the process of life.

You will no longer hold onto regrets, mistakes, and bad decisions. You will grow off the back of them.

Remember: learn, grow, repeat!

13

Just Get to the Next Grade

What are the Cs?

There are three key performance factors that stand out for me as being missing when I'm working with men. But these three qualities are essential pillars for an individual's growth. When you are on top of these qualities, you're able to be much more effective on your mission. So you have to be following and implementing them to see the difference in your own life.

It takes hard work to be on top of all of the Cs, but one without the others can affect your ability to reach your potential. Bringing them together will bind the whole mission together, and connect the dots of what you are trying to accomplish for your long-term focus.

Let's explore them.

C – Consistency

I hear these statements a lot: 'I started the process of changing, but slipped back into bad habits' or 'I just can't keep up the momentum, I'm just not motivated.'

Consistency is the one thing that can really change the game for you, yet it's the one thing that so many people struggle with.

Imagine if I asked you to run 15 miles a day for 12 weeks. Could you consistently do that? The answer is most likely no. It's unsustainable in terms of capabilities, time, managing the body, other commitments, etc.

Now imagine if I asked you to run two miles a day for the next 12 weeks, could you consistently do that? I would say a lot of you could say yes. So, what's the difference?

Running two miles a day is much more realistic in terms of your capabilities, time, and balance with the rest of your life. It's not overwhelming, and is a sustainable process that you could carry out.

Unrealistic outcomes

From my experience of working with thousands of men over the years, many aren't consistent because the outcome they are seeking is unrealistic against their conditioning at that time. That means that the process to get there is unsustainable and an unrealistic ask, making it an inconsistent process. It doesn't fit into the realistic bubble of what can be achieved.

To make something consistent, you must learn to make the small changes (1% better rule), managing them to condition your mind, emotions, and physical state.

Once you've reached a level of consistency at the stage of conditioning you're at, you are then ready to up your game and follow the same process to reach the next level. Where it goes wrong is when you set the bar way too high too soon. Consistency is then affected, the outcome is never achieved, and you slip back to old ways.

When I talk about consistency to my clients, I'm talking about the momentum of action. I'm talking about showing up every day. And that's where the 1% better rule applies. Don't try to change your life overnight, don't look for the quick fixes or the hacks. Let's find consistency in your mission.

All of the strategies and models and tactics I teach are designed to maintain consistency at a controlled level, so that you reach the standard of living, happiness, and fulfilment that you desire.

Being a yo-yo with your implementation, your decision-making, and your life overall, creates nothing but frustration, stress, and low confidence. I've seen hundreds of men fall by the wayside on their journeys because they couldn't maintain consistency and went from there to simply not showing up.

Slipping back into old ways

Most people end up back in the same place when consistency is not achieved. That place where laziness thrives, excuses are rife, unhappiness reigns, and you slip into denial mode again.

Momentum is lost, and you struggle to look yourself in the eye because things have gone backwards. You can't help but feel that you've let yourself down, or are ashamed or embarrassed. That's the power of consistency – or in this case not having consistency.

Understanding what the alternative is when you fail to be consistent should be a constant reminder for you to show up every day, a minimum of 1% a day. You don't want the alternative, because it doesn't serve you.

I know if I stopped being consistent in my life, the wheels would fall off, and I'd end up being that lonely man, drinking again and not thinking of others. I would have undone all of the hard work I've put in to this date. That's why consistency is non-negotiable; the alternative is not a place either you or I want to be.

C – Control

How frustrating is it when you don't have control of your life? I would go as far as saying that the process of not having control is a huge reason why you struggle with your emotions, relationships, health, or career. When I chat to a lot of people, what I can hear is poor control measures.

EXAMPLE:

Sunday night is the classic time when you most feel the effects of not having control of your life. Let's say you are the typical Monday-Friday guy who has weekends off. (If you are a shift worker, then try imagining this scenario on a day when you tend to feel the same way.)

Picture this. You are sitting on your sofa on a Sunday night, it's 18.00, and you've had a lovely weekend with the family or friends. You're still feeling rough from the hangover you had this morning, as you tried to drink away your issues over the weekend, and now you have another beer or glass of wine in hand.

You are dreading going into work tomorrow and going back into the rat race. It's the thought that you have no idea of what is going to happen at work tomorrow: is your boss going to be in a good or bad mood? Or if you are the boss, you're dreading the ball ache of having to get around your staff to give them a boot up the arse. Either way, the uncertainty creates the dread.

In your mind, you cycle through all of the things that you have to do, and become increasingly overwhelmed with the sheer volume of thoughts as you go into overdrive with your overthinking. Your brain starts to feel overloaded, creating high levels of anxiety from the uncertainty. Sounds draining just writing that, let alone experiencing it.

You don't particularly enjoy the process of life, because it just feels so disorganised, and your relationship with Monday means you've got five days straight of the same BS. There's nothing to look forward to, and the thought of firefighting another week leaves you feeling drained and depleted of energy before you even start.

That's a pretty awful situation to be in, right? Now, not every person will feel like that. Some may be worse, some maybe less so, but it's just one example of not controlling your time and energy to be more productive and more in control of how your life will pan out.

What I've learned over the years, as a result of working on myself and others, is that a lack of control in your life is one of the largest contributors to anxiety, mental health, stress, relationship breakdowns, and poor health management issues. So I know it's an essential factor to nail down.

How can you feel more in control?

Essentially, it's a case of you learning to run the show, rather than the show running you. I've found that the best way to attack this is by having better habits, routines, and structure. In my first book, *It's a State of Mind,* I talked a lot about how to plan your time – timetabling your days for the week, to feel more in control of how you spend your time and energy.

Think about it. To manage your bank account, you most likely look at it once a day, maybe three to four times a week. You look at your accounts, at what is going out, what's coming in, and what you've spent. You have the dates of the direct debits that are going out, and when money is due to come in. All of that allows you to balance the accounts so you can afford to live and not flush all of your money down the drain. It's a simple example of a part of your life that you control. Life without that control of your money would mean missed payments, which could lead to losing your home, bad credit, etc.

So, when it comes to managing your time and energy, surely doing the same things will give you balance and guidelines to maintain control?

Let's take the example I gave about Sunday night. Imagine if you were now sitting there at 18.00, but this time with a timetable of the week telling you where your time and energy was going, where you were going to be, at what time, and what was going to be done.

On that timetable and plan, you would have information detailing what you had to do each day to meet your expectations and obligations. For example, when you were going to work out, finish for the day, get up and do your morning routine, etc.

It's just like managing your accounts, but this time the currency is time. And having it all down on paper allows your mind to settle, as you know exactly what's happening rather than second-guessing everything going on in your life. You are now starting to take control.

Seeing the working system

Once you've implemented a control system to manage your time and energy, you'll be focusing on specific tasks rather than flapping around and cuffing each day as it comes, which only leads to your daily firefights. Remember the hamster wheel?

The benefits of this system are huge, especially when it comes to your mental, emotional, and physical well-being. You suffer less overwhelm, less anxiety, less stress, enjoy a clearer mind and better performance at work, home, and in health. Instead of drowning in your overthinking and overwhelm, you now have the tools to keep you afloat.

And yes, of course there are going to be bad days, and times when the plan doesn't get followed. That's just reality. But the difference is how you deal and manage that reality. When you are in control of the situation and your life, you can wake up the next day and just come back to your plan, your mission. You've followed the process, and as a result become much more resilient to the blows.

The alternative is waking up still feeling pissed off, emotional, and even more overwhelmed without the support of your plan, leaving your mind to race and become unproductive and frustrated again.

How does this all link?

When there is a mission in your life, the control elements are essential to taking the 1% steps forward. All of the plans that you create to control your time become very relevant to how you spend your time and energy. In theory, the way you spend your time and energy should align with your mission.

So your mission is a great reference point when reviewing if you are spending your time and energy wisely.

Time and energy spent on people, tasks, or environments that are not parallel with your mission, is in fact wasted time and energy, and could be classed as a distraction. But the element of control becomes refined with practice and process, which means that the more you do this, the more clinical you become in your practice.

On Fridays, I plan the following week. I check that it's all relevant and meeting the missions in my life that I've set myself. Some might consider this as overkill. But I just feel that if you are going to improve the number one asset you own – which is you! – then you can't leave any stone unturned.

After all, you wouldn't neglect the control elements of your bank account, so why would you do that with your main asset?

To become the ultimate version of yourself, you have to have the ultimate control over your time, energy, and your actions.

Having that control has a huge positive impact on your mental, emotional, and physical state.

C – Clarity

There is this little voice that's active in your brain, which constantly presses the doubt button. We've all heard it. You doubt yourself as a father or husband, you doubt your future and where you are heading, you doubt what you are capable of, you doubt if you can change.

Doubt is a habit you've picked up from life – like a virus. You've either been around the wrong people or environments, with poor teachers or parents, and as a result your pattern of thinking has always been to doubt yourself. So, over time you have fallen into the habit of always thinking like that.

The good news is that, just like other bad habits, it's not permanent. It's similar to when you put on weight or take on unhealthy habits, it can be undone through consistent action to control your time and energy in the right places. You just first need the clarity as to what and why you must/want to change.

Doubt, for me, is like the morning sea fog. It gives you limited vision, and it represents what your thoughts look like in your own mind. It prevents you from clearly seeing the path you need/want to take to make the changes you desire. That creates elements of doubt, uncertainty, and confusion about how to tackle your mission, or where your life should go.

The self-doubt is usually an element of fear of failure and overthinking. You'll have thoughts of: *If I put myself on the line and fail, what will others think of me? If I fall flat on my face, how will that make me feel?*

Most thoughts of fear are about worrying about what others think. But that just means you are not at the point of fully accepting yourself as a person, and not comfortable with who you are. When you have clarity of who you are and what you represent, you don't give a shit about what others think; you only focus on your own judgement of yourself.

Finding complete certainty about you and your identity, and what you are trying to achieve, is clarity at the highest level. No one and nothing can then affect your outcome.

Why is clarity so important?

When I went out to Afghanistan and we went on patrol, we had to be absolutely clear on what the mission was. We needed to know the routes, the potential threats, and the SOPs (standard operating procedures). We got this clarity by being given face-to-face orders on the mission.

Imagine if we had been given a piece of paper which explained what the mission was, but with no explanation as to the logistics. That would leave doubts, uncertainty, and questions. I'd want/need clarity that I knew the plan myself, so that if we got into the shit, I knew what the score was. If I didn't, it would make me feel uneasy when on patrol.

Orders in the military are given as a formal presentation and follow a structured format. This can last anywhere from an hour to three, depending on the size of the mission and the number of people to be briefed. Why so detailed? Because every man has to know the plan. There has to be clarity in the operators' minds and in the officers' minds that everyone knows what's happening and when. If one of the leaders is hit, the next man can take over, knowing exactly what's happening. This level of clarity can save someone's life in war, and that's the power of having it. In the same way, having that level of clarity in your own life could save yours.

Let's look at your life. You wake up every morning, unsure what the day's going to bring, when your next workout is going to be, what you are achieving in your life, or what's making you happy.

Many men live their lives like this, completely disconnected from what's going on around them, blinded by the issues. They have just accepted the situation, and just put up with the uncertainty.

Let's discuss the actions that make the difference between those men who suffer with the fog of doubt in their mind and that lack of clarity, and those wakening to having direction and focus, like the set of orders given to us in Afghanistan.

Imagine waking up to a morning routine. A routine that gives you clarity about why you are on a journey, about why you are getting up an hour earlier than normal whilst it's freezing outside, the things you are trying to achieve, connecting with your mission. Imagine knowing what you are trying to achieve from the moment you open your eyes.

Imagine working towards a life mission that would lift

you up to new heights of action, that would allow you to rediscover who you were as a man. A man on a mission to reinvent himself, to eradicate any wrong doings of the past, and to use it as fuel to learn, grow, and repeat.

That is the importance of clarity. Knowing why you MUST show up, rather than SHOULD show up. Understanding the reason you are showing up, and leaving the foggy mind behind.

The three Cs are powerful qualities that will help you align with your mission. The three Cs provides the formula that allows you to keep showing up and managing key components of your growth. They are requirements to be met to ensure you are on track with your mission.

14

Dealing With Regrets

The grading system

If you've ever done martial arts, you'll understand the process of a grading system. As I mentioned earlier, I'm a regular BJJ (Brazilian Jiu Jitsu) participator, and I love the process of the grading system for the following reasons:

Recognition

Whenever I've witnessed someone get their new colour belt as a promotion, I can literally see how much it means to that person; the smile from cheek to cheek says it all. It's not just a belt with a different colour; it's recognition for the time and commitment that has been put into training on the mats.

It's recognition for showing up when it's dark and cold and you don't really feel like showing up, but nevertheless you do. It's recognition of showing up when life is tough and testing you, yet you still managed to be there.

It makes you feel as though you've achieved something in your journey. And it's nice to be recognised, isn't it? It's a great feeling for another human being to look at what you're doing, and say that you deserve to go to the next level.

The military is very much the same. The time and hard work you put in, the experience gained, means you move up the ranks. When I went from a Marine rank to Corporal rank, I was so proud. I was then the leader of seven guys, rather than being one of the guys. They were my responsibility, and it felt great that someone said I was good enough to be in that position.

There's always something to chase

It's very rare to have something to chase in life. If you think of yourself between the years of 18-25, most of you were mainly chasing girls around the pubs and clubs. Maybe some of you were chasing a career.

Think about where you are today: what are you chasing to achieve right now in your life? The beauty of platforms like martial arts and the military is that you are always chasing the next grade, more experience, more challenges.

The process you follow in that chase is what gives you that experience, and you are learning as you go – failing, falling down, and picking yourself up again. And that journey never ends, even at the highest level. When you know what the standard is, reaching your next goal becomes your mission and you will go all in to achieve it with patience, passion, desire, and drive. That is a powerful process in its own right.

What does all of this have to do with you changing?

Why am I talking about martial arts and military ranking?

Well, that's because it has a lot to do with how you progress as a human being. Finding the next level in your chapter – whether it's getting to level 1 or 10 – and understanding the need for progression throughout your life is key to you winning.

Translating this to your life

For many of you reading this book, there will be this huge void following you like a dark shadow. Most of the time you don't know what it is, but you just feel like something is missing. Sometimes it can feel like it's there as soon as you wake up in the morning, and until the time you go to bed. It's like having a huge hole in your chest, and you don't know how to deal with it, or how to fill it.

Some of you have everything you want in life. You can be the envy of all your friends and peers, but still something is missing. What we need to inject into your life is a similar framework to the grading system. You need to know what your next level up is, and you need to focus on achieving that, finding out what it is, and what it'll do for you. You need to understand how it will help you discover you, and your character, values, and principles.

Quite often, that void is a lack of fulfilment. Over the years, I've learned that a lack of fulfilment comes down to a couple of things, and focusing on them has really allowed me to slowly fill the void that was present for so long in my own life.

The feeling of progression

The first thing was the feeling of progression. It's quite an obvious link if you think about my background in the military. I was always working and striving to achieve the next thing, whatever that might have been.

On reflection, I was hungry for experience. Experience, in my mind, was the key to a successful career in the military. I saw so many peers sitting around waiting for opportunities to come to them, but I was taught by my training corporal early on that you get out of your military career what you put in. And that sticks with me today.

When I joined the military, I wanted to be a sniper, and I did that. When I became a sniper, I wanted to teach snipers, and I did that. When I taught snipers, I wanted to be a PTI, and I did that. And when I wanted to be an outdoor instructor, I did that. Just like the grading system, I was always looking for the next progression, the next chapter, the next place I could learn, gain experience, fail, grow, find out more about myself.

And it's that same mindset that I believe can help you!

Giving back

The second thing was very unexpected; it's giving back. I've heard many stories about people I follow who have well established businesses, or are well known public figures, and who have given so much back. And it's one of the reasons I provide so much content. I want to give as much of my experience and knowledge to those who want to listen.

I produce my Rise To Thrive show three times a week, offering half an hour of free content and coaching a week. And the number of emails I receive, telling me how it's helped, has been overwhelming.

There have been guys who have needed a break in life because of financial issues, and I've paid for them to do my course; to date, I've sponsored nearly £15k worth of training to those on their knees over the last six years. Through tough times during the COVID era, I've put on hold many of my most loyal Mastermind clients' payments, to give them a breather yet still be able to be a part of the group. It's made me feel so fulfilled that I've been able to do that for them.

When these guys message to say they can't believe the generosity, it makes me smile. A business isn't just about making an income; it's a mission that should be about practising what you preach for those who need it the most.

Finding fulfilment comes in all shapes and sizes. It could be the look in your wife's eyes when you tell her just how grateful you are to have her; it could be the smile on your kids' faces when you tell them how proud you are of them; it could be the relief on a friend's face when you offer your time to help them when they are struggling. These are scenarios we all take for granted from time to time.

They are my examples. Now what about you? To achieve the next level in your life, the next grade, or rank, or experience, what target are you going to set for yourself?

As humans, we want to feel as though we are moving forwards and not backwards. How can *you* move forwards from today? What tweaks to your life can you make?

I want you to think about your progression. How do you move forwards on the progression train, even if it's only 1% a day, that will satisfy the brain in terms of feeling fulfilled?

How you get to the next grade

There are people who talk a good game and get carried away with the vision of what they can achieve in their head, and others who show up and do what they said they would. Which one of those descriptions best sums you up at the moment? Answer that question in your mind – and don't lie to yourself.

Are you a talker? Or a doer? If you're not sure, the best way to answer this is by looking at the last three months. What have you done to change for good?

In the role of being a coach, I've heard all of the hot air and talk of change. *'This is the first day of my new life, blah, blah.'* I know that probably sounds a little negative, and you might wonder why I'm not being a little more encouraging.

The truth is, mate, being encouraging doesn't do anything other than puff your ego and get your impulses going for all of five minutes. I think a point-blank approach is required when someone is full of shit about what 'they are going to do'. In my experience, it's the preferred approach. Instead of talking, let's see the action!

If you are offended by this way of thinking, you're clearly reading the wrong book and listening to the wrong coach. There are plenty of softer books out there who will tell you it's going to be okay to just talk a good game rather than actually showing up. But, really, it's not!

I'd rather encourage you to take action, or at least try to accomplish what you set out to do, put in some level of effort, and show me you're in it for the long haul.

My own definition of a talker and a doer

Talker: An individual who clearly underestimates what's required to change. Driven by impulse, and continually makes impulse decisions to change.

Many would call this 'being full of shit'. I would call it confused. The individual always turns to making false claims of changing to ease the guilt of not taking action, but it's a method to trick the mind. It satisfies their low feelings for a short period of time. *Saying* that you're going to do something makes you feel like you are doing something about it... until you fail to show up.

You often hear this talk from people after a night out. 'I'm not drinking any more'; 'I'm not doing drugs any more'; 'I'm not sleeping with strangers any more'. It's an instant way to make you feel better, and feel as though you can progress further. Sadly, though, it only creates more frustration for the individual, as it proves time and again that they have no real intention of change. They just like to talk a great game.

It's worth mentioning that not everybody is *ready* to change mentally, emotionally, or physically. Sometimes you just have to find the trigger to make you see the bigger picture. If that's the case, just stop complaining you're not where you want to be, and accept that unless you are ready and willing to change, this is your way of living until that trigger happens.

Doer: An individual who has found a reason to change the way they live their life. Somebody who doesn't necessarily talk about what they are going to do all of the time, but shows intent with action rather than words.

The doer has most likely reached a pinnacle in their life and found a 'must' to change their ways – something that creates emotion and connection to changing. Examples could be nearly losing an important relationship, losing a parent, or hitting rock bottom.

Do you notice the difference between the two? The talkers fail to see their MUST for change and emotional connection to action, while the doer has found a reason, that emotional connection to the mission to make the changes required.

No matter what my skills are as a coach, no matter the advice I give, I can't help to change somebody who is not prepared to change themselves.

I know that a talker will listen to me for ten minutes when I give encouragement, and that nine times out of ten it will fall on deaf ears and no action will be taken. On average, it takes someone six months to decide to invest with me on one of our programmes, from the minute they've found me. That's not necessarily because they don't know me well enough to invest in themselves, but because they haven't found the reason they need to change yet.

I quite often repeat a lot of my key principles and messages, so that at some point, one day someone will turn around and have that moment where it suddenly hits them in the face. It's like Neo in *The Matrix,* when he suddenly sees the Matrix and he just gets it. He sees it. He has the moment... like you do.

TASK:

While it's fresh in your mind, grab a notepad and jot down some ideas about the areas in which you want to progress. What's your first step if you are at the start line? What's the next level if you've just started your journey?

Is it creating a morning routine and time for yourself?

Is it getting home on time and being present when you're there?

Is it getting those consistent workouts in?

Is it finding a way to make your relationship stronger with your wife and kids?

These questions will get the blood flowing, and you will feel like you're taking control of the situation and starting to create some direction and focus. This task will also allow you to concentrate fully on the priorities and areas of your life that need attention right away.

Are you going to say you'll do this later? Or are you an action-taker and are going to do it now?

The ball's in your court.

15

You Are the Priority

The priority pyramid

The priority pyramid. Two models that tell you exactly where you are on the list of your own priorities.

Bottom of the pile

Model A is where the individual is at the bottom of the priority pyramid, with work being the biggest priority, and his own health being the furthest away of the priorities. This model shows that the individual is carrying the weight of the world on his shoulders. He's most likely obligated to his work, and has been sucked into misplacing his priorities.

If this is you, you are not alone in dealing with this situation. I've worked with thousands who allow the chaos of work to be the priority and to take over. Many base their lives around their career, and not their career around their lives.

Someone who is in this position is most likely burnt

out, both mentally and emotionally. Overwhelmed, firefighting, rapidly losing their own identity, and out of sorts in terms of the direction in which they're heading – if indeed there is any direction right now.

Everyone and everything will most likely come before you do. You are right at the back when it comes to you as a priority, and it's almost impossible to say no. And because you are in so deep, you feel there is no way out of this rut or series of patterns that have formed in your thought process in the way you have been living your life.

What I'd like to highlight here is that there is no shame in being in this spot. You aren't the only one, and you won't be the last. Somehow, you've just slipped into this state of mind and this pattern of actions. Usually, it's due to a drive to want to provide for your family, or sometimes it's just the pressure you've been put under by your employer.

But you slipped into this rut, so you can slip out of it. It is not a permanent status, and it's not terminal – as long as you are ready to try and get out of it! You are in complete control of your mind, your body, and your decisions, so you can do this. But you have to want to do it!

On top

Model B is when the individual is at the very top of the pyramid. This shows that he is putting himself before everyone and everything going on in his life. He is ready to put his oxygen mask on before anyone else's.

If this is you, then you are showing up at a much higher level of awareness of what is going on around you. You are conscious of the problems, you become more consistent, and you have more control and clarity of where your life is going.

I tend to find that when you have found a mission in life, and recognise that to achieve that mission you must ensure you are the priority, everything below you in the pyramid gets the best version of you.

Getting to this position, however, takes a lot of work and commitment. It takes persistence and consistency – like anything that's worth having. Most people that reach this state realise the power of the growing 1% a day every day forever mentality; they are patient and understand that the micro-wins are essential to achieve the long-term mission.

Being in love with the process is what is going to get you to the top of the pyramid. Desire, passion, drive, and connection to your mission, are what will keep you there.

Carrying the weight of the world

I've got to pay the bills, I've got to support the family, I've got to be a good dad, I've got to perform in my job, I've got to work longer and later, I have to give my family the lifestyle they want, I've got to keep fit, I've got to say yes to all opportunities, I can't look weak, I have to look confident... Fuck me, dude!

These are just some of the self-pressures I'm hearing

you put on yourselves, and I hear them all of the time through my programmes. The constant barrage of overthinking is crippling you, and it's destroying your self-confidence to the point where you are becoming hampered by anxiety, low moods and, in the worst cases, suffering suicidal thoughts.

You carry all of that emotionally, mentally, and physically, everywhere you go, like a rucksack. It's weighing you down like the bergen sack I mentioned earlier.

Without that rucksack weighing you down, the capabilities you have are endless. You have no idea of what an incredible human being you are. You just don't have the training or conditioning yet to realise that, nor do you have the confidence or self-belief to see it. But that will come through a lot more as you start to work on yourself, and the more you work on yourself the more self-assured you can be.

You are most likely firefighting problems and distractions daily, overthinking, and putting yourself last in the list of priorities. You just don't have that training or conditioning yet to manage and control your life, but it will come.

Rediscover yourself

In some respects, you have to learn to live again, to re-educate yourself, your brain, and your patterns of thought, and there's nothing wrong with that. I started the process as I came out of my turmoil. I rediscovered myself through self-learning, growing, and repeating the process, doing courses and being part of positive communities.

I left formal education 22 years ago, but I know it's vital to constantly keep teaching and pushing myself (a minimum of 1% a day), learning and experiencing. It's important to understand that self-learning and personal development is about being better in your own mind, in your own skin, taking more control, and loving the process more. That's the mission, right? To live a better way, because living the way you are right now isn't working.

I often think of those recruits who used to come through Royal Marine training when I was a PTI. These boys – and they were just boys – were filled with ambition, drive, and desire to earn the right to wear the coveted green beret.

These boys had no idea what they were capable of until the training team drove them to their absolute limits, until they were pushed emotionally, mentally, and physically, so far out of their comfort zones. For those few who eventually made it, the results were to live a life of passion, pride, and vision, in a very special brotherhood who wore the same green beret that united us all.

I don't want *you* to be a Royal Marine, but I do want you to be an Elite Operator in your own life. And to do that, sacrifices are going to have to be made. You are going to have to change your current way of thinking and acting if it's not benefiting you and those around you. And you need to see things more clearly, without ego, temptation, and distraction, in order to work your way up that priority pyramid.

My man, when you get there, to that point where you suddenly feel in control of your life again and stay there, you'll be so proud of yourself! You'll see the world from a different point of view, one you've not seen in years – if ever.

Being at the bottom of your priority pyramid means there is only one way from here, so what are you waiting for?

When you're on top

I want you to visualise finally being at the top of that priority pyramid. How do you feel mentally, emotionally, and physically? If you haven't been there, it can be very hard to picture, but try using your imagination. This could be your mission.

Let me explain the idea of you being at the top of your priority list, so that I can help you visualise it. This isn't a right or wrong approach, but it's from my experience of seeing life on the other side of doom and gloom, and one I've used to help many men.

Health: When you are at the top of the priority pyramid, your health becomes part of your lifestyle. It's an automatic routine and process. There's no negotiating the run, or the gym session, or the morning routines, and you naturally start to handle stress better, the environments around you, and the punches in the face.

Mental, emotional, and physical well-being all come

under health, and your habits, routines, and structure all create the three Cs I spoke about earlier in the book (Consistency, Control, Clarity).

The three Cs, the routines, showing up, all prime you for a better way of living, a higher level of thinking, and much more control. You give yourself a much better chance to keep your head above water when the tidal wave of life comes crashing in. This, in effect, has huge benefits over the other three pillars as well.

So, staying on top of your health 99.9% of the time sees the other three pillars fall into place, because you are thinking clearer.

Relationships: You've put yourself first mentally, emotionally, and physically, and now you are in the Elite Operator state of mind. The by-product of you being a better version of yourself is that you have a higher level of self-awareness to communicate and understand better in your close relationships.

When you are putting you first, you're a better husband or partner, you are a better dad or friend, you are a better brother or sister. But when you allow the weight of the world to take over your emotions and mental state, you are too distracted to see things clearly, which usually results in a short-tempered or distracted husband or dad.

How many times have you snapped at everyone at home? How many times have you failed to ask your parents how they are? How many times have you not been present with your kids?

Why? Because you are firefighting life, in the hamster wheel of doom, too short-sighted to have the awareness of what's going on right in front of you. The lack of emotional conditioning and patience causes you to hit nuclear, and you take your anger out on all of the people around you who have done nothing wrong.

I understand that this will be hard to hear or deal with. But the truth often is. It's better to hear the truth now and deal with it than having to cope with your partner leaving you because it's too difficult to live with you.

The fact of the matter is, when you are the best version of yourself, everybody else in your life gets that best version of you. You are nicer to be around, more understanding, more helpful, and less of a massive cock!

Personal development: Personal development in itself is raised when you are putting yourself first. In fact, personal development is more than likely the thing that got you to the top of your priority pyramid and will keep you there.

When you are in that place, the need to grow and expand your horizons almost becomes addictive. You consume new ways of thinking, new mindsets and approaches to life. You listen to more audiobooks and podcasts, you register for courses, you read books, take part in programmes, and find ways to improve this new, re-energised man. It then becomes a matter of how far you can progress.

This becomes an automated factor in your life, meaning that it's a lifestyle! It's part of the mission you are on, it's the rocket fuel, it's the path that you've identified and are following. And you realise that in order to achieve the mission, you have to constantly keep evolving by continually self-developing and learning.

Business: For me, this is the biggest shift in your state of mind. You have now come to terms with the fact that life doesn't equal work. Yes, you have to work, and you recognise it brings its challenges along the way, but it no longer consumes you or controls you. You no longer become the burnt-out train wreck you were before, and you no longer see yourself as a slave to the system.

In fact, because you have now become a lot more focused on yourself, your performance in your career has risen, time management and energy levels are higher, productivity is through the roof, and you are able to leave work at work. You've become a lot more clinical and efficient with the tasks you have to complete, you are able to handle problems, and decision-making is a lot easier.

Why work isn't the priority

If you don't work, there's no money, then there's no roof over your head, no bills are paid. I get that, but it's not the priority.

Don't confuse what I'm telling you here, though. I'm not telling you not to work, or to mug work off like it's something that's not important. It *is* important. But you spend a large amount of your life working, so whatever you do has got to be enjoyable. There surely has to be an element of passion to the job, some ambition, some form of challenge or thirst to excel. Can you imagine spending 20-30 years in a job that slowly crushes your soul? Going to work in a job you hate can be like eating dry cereal every morning – it's very unpleasant and is difficult to swallow.

Seriously, I've worked with numerous men in the corporate world, in the building trade, in other professions, entrepreneurs, etc. – all of whom have had the life sucked from them. They've sacrificed the extra hours to meet demands that are forced upon them. They've felt obligated to do more than they should, and they've been unable to say NO. They've become the fucking 'YES man'.

A slave to the system

I've seen men who have had every shred of energy drained from them mentally, emotionally, and physically, as they became a slave to the employer or their own work obsession. The sacrifice becomes the broken marriage and poor relationship with their children. The sacrifice becomes their mental health, the overwhelm, the chronic fatigue, exhaustion, and burnout.

They become a zombie that eats, sleeps, works, repeats... then men wonder why they are dead inside, why the flame has disappeared. Their patterns of thought, mindset, dreams, and ambitions have become a toxic wasteland with no room for growth!

Working overtime becomes the obligation, and many sacrifice time for money, feeling obliged to give their family a certain lifestyle. So many men feel like they have to sacrifice themselves to provide for others, and all that fucking bullshit!

They take the promotion and become the 12-14 hours-a-day guy, with every ounce of energy squeezed from them to earn every penny of the promotional increase. And it's not even their business! They are giving their work all their time and energy – in essence, their life.

When it comes to the end of your career, and you get a handshake and a shitty gold pen, do you think that everything you sacrificed – health, relationships, missed moments with the kids – was worth it?

Sure, you'll have a pension, but will you have a life? Maybe you will, maybe you won't, but is it a risk you're willing to keep taking?

I've heard more than enough grown men cry down the phone to me because their wife left them for someone who was actually paying attention to them, rather than sitting next to their distant husband on his laptop writing emails or finishing reports. Or because their husband walked through the door late night after night, and she had to explain to the kids why Daddy had to work all of the time, rather than having a meaningful relationship.

Hard to read? Good. Suck it up, because you still have a chance to change this outcome!

Still think work is the priority?

Here's another curveball! You grab your left arm and the unbearable pain going through your chest alerts you to the fact that you are having a heart attack.

You've become so tense, so stressed, you've neglected your health so much, that you are now on a cliff edge of either dying and leaving your world behind, or being in a position where you can't work!

My father passed when he was 40 because of his lifestyle. He left me at five years old, when I needed him the most, and my mum had to pick up the pieces. I was left with an arsehole of a stepdad who emotionally bullied me for ten years!

I'm not angry at the decisions my dad made, and I'm not angry he was ambitious. I'm just sad I never got to know him, or to introduce him to my first girlfriend, to be reassured when I was first dumped, have our first beer together, have him at my wedding, have him watch me pass out of Royal Marine training, be a grandad to my kids. Remember the ripple effects of misplacing your priorities!

So, open your fucking eyes, and wake the fuck up! What are you sacrificing by making your work the priority, and killing yourself in the process?

Work isn't the priority. It's the killer of most good men because they become consumed and dominated by it. Be great at your job, but get the balance right.

You are the priority, the asset. And you have to be,

because if you are not, how can you possibly manage your work/life balance and not let work take over?

It's not selfish

The biggest resistance to putting yourself first is the overwhelming feeling that you are being selfish.

Here's the official meaning of selfish: *Lacking consideration for other people, devoted to or caring for oneself.*

Now, let's put into perspective the act of putting yourself first. I'm not saying that you should live like a single man in a bachelor pad, ignoring all responsibilities, and life's pressures. That *would* be selfish, and it would be a one-way ticket to divorce or being single, or isolating yourself from your friends.

And if you don't have kids and are single, I'm not saying that you have to ignore your friends and family in order to focus on yourself.

I simply want you to understand that by putting some time into yourself, you are actually going to be giving more to others.

This process or state of mind doesn't take a great deal of time, either. We are talking about pockets of time that allow *you* to be the focus of your attention. In these pockets of time, you will dedicate yourself to your mental, emotional, and physical self-care.

You'll spend time developing habits, routines, and structure that improve and master your emotional responses, your understanding of things you control, putting factors of your life into perspective. But these periods of time shouldn't be perceived as selfishness; they're acts that benefit you and your surroundings. And I believe it's vital to communicate and help others that are close to you to understand about your mission, what you are trying to achieve, and why.

Too many men don't share the struggles they go through with those closest to them, for fear of judgement, through feelings of embarrassment, or by being ashamed. But these people are the ones who should be caring about you the most, so explain to them that you are trying to make a difference. If they love you or care for you, they'll understand! Let me expand on this.

Communication and understanding

Many men reading this book won't have an understanding of how to put themselves first or what that actually means. Some won't know how to get the balance right, while others will dismiss this mindset and say it's not realistic.

As I've just said, one of the most important factors in starting this process is to communicate clearly what the plan is to those around you that will be affected – your wife, friends, family, kids, whoever is relevant. The purpose for this communication is so that they have a clear understanding of what you are trying to achieve, what your mission is currently in life, and the reasons you're doing it. Some won't understand, some will be negative, while others will encourage you.

Anything I've ever done in the last seven years, I've always explained to my partner. Why? Because I want her to know why I'm getting up at 04.15 in the morning. I want her to know what I am doing and why I'm doing it. That way, she can get on board with it.

She knows now that the morning routine is a vital part of my day to achieve a better version of myself. We both recognise that without me taking part in the morning routine, I'm a nightmare to be around. I'm agitated, unfocused, and moody. No doubt, you know all the symptoms by now.

But thanks to the clear communication, she gets it. She understands me. Not just the morning routine, but the whole routine and the mission I'm on. And equally, I get what she needs in order to maintain a level head and happiness in her own life. We are best mates first, and you should always be able to open up and communicate with your best mate.

How to put yourself first

What's essential here is to understand that everybody will do this differently. The way I do it will be different to somebody else, and that's what makes us human. The way we see the world and the factors we set as a priority might be different, but we all want the same outcome – to live a better life.

In my case, I set aside uninterrupted time between 04.15 and 07.00. That's my morning ritual, following a process of habit and routine to form a structure in which each element has a micro purpose.

Each factor of that morning routine plays a part in how I mentally, emotionally, and physically prepare for the day. There's a system, and it works for me. And the beauty of it is that I'm not sacrificing family time, or work time, to do this.

Sure, when I first began getting up early, it caused slight disruption with my partner's sleep, but because we had the communication and understanding, she knew the long-term plan.

After a while, she adapted, and now doesn't even stir when I get up. It's evolving the process, and things that used to seem different just become normal. Now, when I get up at 04.15, it's no different to when I got up at 07.00. I'm still tired and bleary-eyed. But I just have an extra 2 hours 45 minutes to get ahead of the day.

Building from the morning up

That time in the morning is the time that I need to help develop me as the priority, to prime and prepare myself for what the day is going to bring. Not many of us have much time to be able to focus on ourselves during the day, so in my first book I talked about this as the Golden Hour.

It's simply setting a period of time where you prioritise

you. The Golden Hour is an hour to yourself to grow, learn, and develop, a powerful system to slowly, at 1% a day, push you up the priority pyramid.

The by-product of finding this time is that men can eat better, reduce drinking because they build better controlling mechanisms, increase the level of performance at home, work, and health, build awareness of their own emotions, mindset, and the ripple effects of their actions. The list could go on, but I'm sure you get the point. These are positive by-products of putting yourself first.

This process also links up nicely with the 1% better a day rule, and remembering the mission. To achieve the mission, you have to remain in and around the top end of the priority pyramid. And the way you do that is by getting 1% better a day by putting yourself first, so that everyone else reaps the benefits of the best version of you. It's the process, it's long-term play, it's remoulding the way you do things.

16

Failing Forwards

Your relationship with failure

Most people I come across have a negative relationship with failure. Many see it as a bad thing, and miss the opportunity that failure brings into their lives. Many are actually crippled by the thought of failure and the damage it can have on their self-image. That fear of judgement and criticism from failure can leave many guys stalling on action, and it's a common cause of procrastination.

My relationship with failure used to be the trigger for my own self-pity and victim mentality. I would fail somewhere along the way, then allow that failure to represent me as a person and what I stood for, i.e. being a failure in life, not feeling good enough, feeling like a reject, as though I was out of my league.

I'd then feel sorry for myself for failing. I'd dwell on the failures and be almost too afraid to go back to trying again, in case I failed again. I allowed it to seriously knock my confidence and consume my mood.

The sniper test

One of the biggest turning points in my life when it came to failure was on the Royal Marine Commando sniper course in October 2005.

The second and third week of the course consisted of long- and short-range shooting tests, and both skills would be tested at the end of the practice week. It was awesome being on that range, and it was what excited me at that time of my career. First, we practised the long-range skills, and all week I was smashing it. I was right up there with the top scorers, and getting to grips with the new weapon system really well.

But when it came to test day, I failed miserably. Maybe I overthought it, buckled under the pressure, or just had an off day. Who knows? But the drive home from Pirbright near London was a long one. I was inconsolable and felt miserable all weekend. I couldn't shake off the negative feeling, and worried about failing again the following week.

After the weekend, though, I was able to get a grip on myself. I went into the short-range practice with the mindset that I was going to smash it, and I did. I had the second highest score of that phase, which was a real confidence boost. Now it all came down to my re-test on the long-range shoot.

My whole career was at a sliding door moment. If I failed this and had to go back to my unit, my draft would have finished in Plymouth, and I'd have been shipped off to Scotland for a security draft that didn't offer many career aspirations. I'd have to face all of the guys, knowing I had failed and had to come off course early. That would have been really hard to take.

However, if I could pass this and get it on my CV, it would open up huge doors for me in my military career.

I really can't explain to you just how nervous I was. My stomach was in bits, my mind frazzled, and I was shaking with adrenaline. The pressure was much more than the actual test. There were just four of us on the re-test, and all eyes were on us. The weather was horrendous, and I knew I had to find that positive mentality.

After thirty minutes of intense test conditions and difficult weather, I passed. Of the four of us on the re-test, two failed – and I won't forget the look on their faces. I know that could easily have been me, if I had kept that negative attitude.

Afterwards, I got in the car and cried with relief. All of that pressure I had carried around from failing the week before came bursting out. I hadn't yet passed the full course – just the shooting phase – but I was so made up to be able to continue to the skill phase.

My whole life, in some respects, could have gone in a completely different direction if I hadn't passed that shoot. Who knows where I would have ended up? But I went on to pass the whole course, and my role of sniping became the foundation to building my career.

Your relationship with failure is the making or breaking of you. So, if you understand it, and embrace it, it can be the making of you, dude.

Fear of failure

In the back of my mind, I failed that initial long-range shooting test because of fear of failure, and I believe that's what caused the overthinking and self-pressure. I was so afraid to fail that my mind had become consumed with failure. It was like treading on eggshells because of that fear, and it prevented me from reaching my potential. I was too afraid to make a mistake, so became stiff and foggy-minded.

But my relationship with fear changed after that. Whenever it came to tests, or challenges in my career and life, I would always think how fear of failure had been such a huge block for me passing that shoot. And I always use that scenario to put perspective on any situation I'm faced with today. The experience gave me so many learning points to improve myself for the future.

Reflecting on that course, I realised that I no longer saw failure as a bad thing, or as a negative. I had heaped so much pressure on myself beforehand because of the consequences of failure. But actually it wasn't the failing that proved to be so negative, as the *fear* of failing. And that experience proved to be a really enlightening moment for me.

The truth is that everyone fails. It happens all of the time, with me, you, your friends, and family.

Fear of judgement

I realised that I was afraid of what people would think if I did fail. Peeling back the layers, it came down to the fact that I didn't want to be perceived as a failure by my peers and officers, yet I was missing the importance that failure was in fact character-building.

I was actually more fearful of what people would think of me than the failing itself. When I look at this scenario today, with a different way of viewing the world, I realise that if I had failed I would have just adapted to whatever new path had come my way. At the time, it was unthinkable to fail. But some 15 years on, I know it really wouldn't have mattered. Sure, maybe for a week or two it would have hurt, but I would have accepted I wasn't good enough on the day, and evolved to what was next.

That belief comes down to not worrying what others think of me any more. Can you imagine me writing this book now if I had the same mentality as back then? I'd never release the book for fear of what everyone would think of me.

Now I am prepared that there will be shit reviews, probably saying they threw it in the bin after the first six pages (lol!), as that seemed to be the theme of my 1-star fan club on the first book. And some will say that the first book was better. But that's just the way the world works.

Does that mean I've failed? Not to me. As far as I'm concerned, I've won. In my head, I've succeeded, and I'm comfortable with what I've achieved. How can I have failed by writing two books? If only I could show my English teacher who said I'd amount to nothing.

Does it mean I've failed if I listen to negative feedback? No, because it doesn't matter; it's not a failure. It just means I've learnt a little more about how the human mind works, how I react to negative feedback, the way that I write, and what positive influence I can have on people. If I save one life or family by someone seeing the truth as it is, then I've won again!

I've turned that fear of failure, fear of what others think of me into my daily fire, and channelled it into what I have learned to help me grow beyond my limits. Now you must do the same!

It's how you learn

Learn, grow, repeat – you know the mantra. That's what I say to myself now whenever something goes wrong, no matter what level it's at. I'm actually looking to fail more often, which sounds like a reckless statement, but let me explain.

The more I try things, push my comfort zones, and explore new avenues, the more open I am that I may fail. But by failing more, I'm actually exposing myself to learning more, and that way I grow from experience. If I repeat that process, I'm constantly moving forwards on my journey in life, through the experience of following a process.

Imagine if I never tried anything – or if you didn't – but carried on firefighting through day-to-day life, just getting by. If we didn't push ourselves, or try to get out of a bad situation, we'd just stay the same. We'd remain in this situation where we would never expose ourselves to failure.

Win or lose, you will always learn and grow. The only time you don't win is when you don't show up or learn from failures because you can't grow when you stay in the fear-of-failure bubble or never learn from experiences.

Think of some of the areas in your life that you constantly consider changing. It might be your health, a new job, maybe it's a side hustle you've been wanting to start. Why haven't you started yet? Why are you procrastinating?

Don't tell me: you're waiting for the right time to get started, the 'someday' mindset. Or is the truth that you are too afraid you're going to fail and fall flat on your face?

I dare you to make a decision today that is going to benefit your life, and follow up with it. Win or lose, I want you to learn from the experience, because the more paths you go down and fail, the closer you are to finding the right path for you. It's how you find your mission, by dipping your toe in lots of different paths available to you.

Try one path; if it's not right, you now know you don't want that in your life or that it's not for you. You try another path, and it suits you better. Test and adjust, as I say. You won't be able to do that sitting on your arse.

Failing forwards

Think about when you go to the gym. When you start lifting weights, what happens is that you begin to tear microfibres of that muscle. When they mend, they come back stronger.

When you see these big dudes lifting heavy weights, with their huge muscles and frames, they have gone through a process over time that in theory seems like you're hurting the body, but it's actually making you stronger.

That's a bit like how I see failing forwards. Many of the fails you'll have over your lifetime will condition you, making you stronger and more resilient to what day-to-day life will throw at you. The failing is like the lifting phase in the gym; it's the process that breaks you down.

The re-forming stronger is down to you – and that's where remembering the mission comes in. A body builder, or anyone committed to having a defined physique, will have sore muscles, and they'll experience days when they don't feel motivated to lift, or to show up, or to follow a very strict diet.

The difference, though, is that they will remember the mission of why they are doing these things; they'll have that emotional connection to improving their physique, or simply maintaining it. And it's that same type of mindset you must adapt if you want to stay on top.

Why do you want to be better?

Many will fail and slip back into the rat race of life, talking about how they were once fit, or used to be in a really good place. From what I've witnessed, people give up on themselves too easily and allow life pressures to topple them. As a result, they fall back 1% rather than forward.

They forget the mission – if there ever was a mission. For many of those individuals, change will never happen. The constant firefighting of life will consume them till the day they die. They choose to think it'll happen one day, or when they'll get around to it, and that's the sad reality of the world we live in today. It's not until you face the consequences of your neglect over the years that you realise you've been on the wrong path.

Don't believe me? Try asking all the 60-year-olds who've been on the phone to me, and who live in a world of regret. It's heart-breaking to hear them say, 'I should've done this or that.'

I often feel that I would never have changed if I hadn't gone through a period of suffering myself. Suffering through failure enabled me to create a 'must' do attitude, rather than an I 'should' do attitude.

Nobody wants to do anything with an I 'should' attitude. Should is like an afterthought; there's a lack of commitment in that word. I 'must' means that it's got to be done, under any circumstances.

Here are a couple of examples:

I *should* lose weight before my blood pressure gets too high.
I *must* lose weight before my blood pressure puts my heart under pressure and I'm at risk of having a heart attack.
I *should* pay more attention to my wife.
I *must* pay more attention to my wife, because she'll end up leaving me if I don't give her the attention she deserves.

One statement is a moment of impulse, a thought that will come and go. The other has consequences of why change has to happen; it adds a connection, a meaning, and an emphasis to what you are saying.

I'd encourage you to fail as frequently as possible, to fail forwards every day. No one builds muscles if they don't do the lifting, and no one in life learns if they aren't showing up.

It's now down to you to show the fuck up, put your ego to the side, and think about the consequences of staying the way you are now! You and your Elite Operator now need to make sure you find your mission.

Summary

I'm not a guru or a life coach. In fact, I absolutely hate those words. Anyone having the balls to call themselves a guru is full of shit in my eyes; it's an ego trap. Many of those figures out there are people who are unwilling to show you what's really happening in their lives. They think they know it all and talk a good game, but they aren't living it through and through.

The 'influencers' that you watch or listen to won't always practise what they preach, but you don't get to see that, so you build up this picture of them having their shit squared away. That's where I'm different. I like to tell and show you my flaws and speed bumps because I don't want you thinking you're not up to somebody else's standard. I don't want you comparing yourself to me or to anyone else. This is your fucking journey, so measure yourself against your own standards. You just need to ensure your standards are high enough for *you*.

Don't look at others and try to become them. This is about your mission and becoming the Elite Operator of your life. So I'm not trying to create a following of JBs, where you all feel you have to get up at 04.15. I just want you to win, but to do that by being you, a 100% you, using some of the tools you've learnt.

I am not a guru because I don't have all of the answers for you; sometimes I don't do what I set out to do. I fail daily in some sort of way. But what I do have is a state of mind, an opinion based on experience of being on the planet for over 40 years, having worked with many men and had meaningful conversations with probably thousands. There's not much I haven't heard.

I feel that it's important for me to share my failures as well as my wins. After all, I am only a human being – a dad, a partner, a friend, son, and brother. I'm no different from you. We all have a story, and many people have been through a lot worse than me. I'm sure we've all experienced something that's shaped and defined our lives. If you haven't, maybe one day you will go through a difficult patch, but at least now you will realise that you are not alone, and you have the tools and mentality to overcome that tough period.

My role is to make an impact on your life in a positive way. I want to do that simply by sharing my experiences, thought processes, case studies, passion, and desire for you to win, and to share my own personal opinion on the world facing men today.

I do that through my Daily Vlog on YouTube, my Rise To Thrive show on The Man Coach Facebook page, and in my podcast It's a State of Mind.

I don't genuinely believe that I can change you by you reading one book. But I hope I've taught you that *you* are the only person who has the power to make a change in your life. No one can ever be the complete package because you should always be hungry for more, and thriving to constantly evolve to reach new levels and new standards through the chapters of your life. It's an evergreen process until you take your last breath in life, then you pass on the torch by leaving your legacy.

I hope I've taught you that you are an incredible human being, despite what you think of yourself, your mistakes and failures, and the pain you keep putting yourself through by dwelling on what you have done. The past doesn't define you; it creates you… if you allow it to.

For me, it's absolutely essential that you have a mission in your life. Having a mission allows you to practise consistency, control, and clarity in your everyday life. It gives you a purpose to wake up in the morning, and it gives you excitement when going to bed that you'll wake up and dive straight into your mission the next day.

A mission is the process, the journey, the experience, the making of you, the forming of an identity. But, hopefully, you now understand that creating a mission isn't always clear cut to start with. Sometimes you have to explore new avenues and approaches to find the right mission that's right for you, so you must be patient.

Remember: If you fail a little, you'll learn a little; learn a little to grow a little. Learn – Grow – Repeat.

And that's where the 1% better a day, every day, forever rule comes into play for you and your mission. Instead of trying to achieve your mission in one week, understand that this is a life project and won't be achieved in a short time.

Micro-wins over time lead to huge wins, and those huge wins are what create you and your identity, as you learn exactly who you are and what you stand for, building values, principles, and character.

Building 1% better wins along the way is a manageable strategy in a chaotic world, and helps you find consistency, control, clarity, and structure. It leads to higher levels of emotional, mental, and physical well-being for you.

This all leads to you understanding that *you* are the priority. And the ripple effect of you being the best version of yourself is better relationships, higher levels of self-awareness, higher performance in the work place, a better work/life balance, and so on.

All these steps are created to simply try and make you happier and more fulfilled in your life. But as I've mentioned a few times, I'm adamant that there are two rules to taking part in any of the courses I run:

1) Show the fuck up every day – no excuses. NONE!
2) Meet me halfway

You can read every self-help book there is – and there's a lot! You can take part in plenty of courses and go to seminars, but unless you are ready to change, unless you are prepared to meet someone halfway, unless you are prepared to show up and commit to the hard work ahead of you, it will all fall on deaf ears.

There isn't a day when I don't think back to sitting on the bed that night while I contemplated taking my life. And I often wonder what life would have been like for my kids if I had; if anybody would even remember me today.

It's a daunting thought, and one that regularly anchors me – my alternative life if I hadn't shown up. Every morning, when I write the three things I'm most grateful for on that day, my first is always that I didn't take my own life, and that I'm alive. That I now have two more little ladies in my life, as well as my big two keeping me active. And that I've found someone special to share my life with.

I look at the impact I've made on the lives of the men who have come into my world, and I feel proud of that. I'm proud of the first business I created by myself, at a time when I was on the verge of losing my house, and losing everything, including my sanity.

And I'm proud of the man I've become today, and the way I handle my mental and emotional states from day to day.

I never used to tell myself those things, but a little self-acknowledgement goes a long way to building your own identity and confidence. I could never say it because of my past and the way I was, but now I'm comfortable to say I'm proud of myself.

Whenever I have a day when I think the storm is coming in, or I forget the mission, I always ask myself: what's the alternative? The alternative is being dead, having never reached my potential in life, and having never fulfilled my mission to create a legacy for my children and the world.

What's the alternative to you not acting on your life?

Isn't it time to create the first chapter of *your* new life?

I wish you every success and luck in creating your masterpiece and building your number one asset – YOU! Remember the mission!

See you on the other side.

JB x

About the Author

James Boardman is a former Royal Marine Commando Sniper and Physical Trainer. He served for a total of nine years, and during that time was deployed to Afghanistan as part of a six-man sniper team. James finished his career as a Sergeant in the Royal Marines. The last four years of his service was spent developing Royal Marine recruits at physical, mental, and emotional levels, ensuring they were ready to go to war straight out of training. During this time, he was responsible for passing out thousands of recruits and managing their physical development.

In 2011, James left the Royal Marines to pursue a family life. He wanted to be present for his two children at the time, and to be there as they grew up. The first three years were unforgiving, as James struggled to come to terms with being back in a normal life, away from the military. Conflicting identities caused him to turn to drink, allowing his family life to crumble, while he fell into a deep pit of insecurity, depression, and constant anxiety.

Within three years, James was divorced, on the verge of losing his house, and struggling to find a path. Minutes away from attempting suicide, he managed to pull himself away from this environment long enough to see a new path. It all started with a run to clear the mind, to wake up and realise what he was about to do. And it worked. This was James's turnaround moment, the pinnacle point where he would shift the way he lived his life.

From there, James grew his character, values, and principles, and through this process developed his identity.

In 2013, James started his first business, which was a fitness bootcamp. Never having run a business before or knowing what to do, James rallied and grew his company to earning £100k in its first year. The process completely transformed James's identity, and a new man was born. Thriving for success, James worked on himself, his controllables, and his mission in life.

In 2017, James started The Man Coach, with the sole purpose of helping men to become Elite Operators in life.

He wanted to help men who were in the same position as he had been when leaving the military, and for others who were simply struggling through life, unsure of who they were, and in what direction they were heading. James's mission became about leaving a legacy to men who needed some form of guidance, mentorship, and leadership.

Leading from the front, James strives every day to challenge men to reach their best selves. In 2020, he started a new company called Time Domination, to help business owners overcome time and energy management issues, and to reach high levels of productivity with sufficient balance between their personal and professional lives.

James lives with his partner Jemima, and has three children – aged 15, 13, and three – and a new little arrival, born July 2021.

Acknowledgements

My family – Jemima, Angelina, Bailey, Alba, and Darci – you are all my mission, my North Star.

My mum, for having to endure years of pain after losing my dad, bringing me and my brother up alone, and for setting what's right and wrong in my life. I love you.

My closest friends, for always being straight with me and telling me how it is.

My mentor and good friend Phil Harrison. Always patient, you have helped me to create a business and mindset that's allowed me to support my mission in life. You make me see everything more clearly.

Cassie for helping me get this book started, and giving me the straight talk when needed.

Every man whose life I've touched, helped, or mentored over the years. It's been an honour.

My staff and ambassadors. You guys do so much good work and play a huge role in changing lives.

The crew of my Mastermind – working with you gives me energy and drive, and you make me want to show up every day.

It's a State of Mind book

No matter how jaded and frustrated you feel, there is a way to lead a more fulfilling life. Find out how with this frank and life-changing audiobook.

This audiobook is specifically for men who are struggling in life right now. The overwhelming chaos of life is almost unbearable, and amongst it all you're neglecting yourself.

Many men wake up one day and wonder how their life has turned into a disaster zone, full of responsibilities and obligations, with no time to truly have fun and be themselves.

How much longer are you going to keep waking up to 'Groundhog Day' and keep telling yourself you'll do something about it on Monday?

This audiobook helps you see why your life has gone off the rails and how you can reclaim a brighter future.

Discover how to:

- Audit your life
- Understand the cause of your unhappiness

- Prioritise and structure your day-to-day routine to improve your well-being
- Use regular small short-term goals to make big changes in your life

Contact James

Via email at me@boardmanjames.com

Facebook at The Man Coach

Instagram at the_man_coach

LinkedIn: James Boardman